Delayed Gratification

by

Nghetlenge Case Ngobeni

Delayed Gratification

Published by

Nghetlenge Case Ngobeni
Dept. of Education-Circuit Off Bldg
Cnr Magistrate Offices and DCO Offices
99 Bankuna Street
Nkowankowa Township, Tzaneen Limpopo Province 0870
South Africa

casengobeni@yahoo.com

Edited by

William Jenkins
4036 Pine Street
Burnaby BC V5G 1Z5
Canada
williamhenryjenkins@gmail.com
http://williamjenkins.ca
Cell: 1-778-928-6139

ISBN-13 978-0-620777-43-8 Paperback South Africa
ISBN-13 978-1-928164-35-7 Paperback Canada
ISBN-10 1928164358 Paperback Canada
ISBN-13 978-1-928164-36-4 Electronic Canada

Delayed Gratification

Delayed Gratification

Contents

Author Nghetlenge Case Ngobeni

About the Author

Mr. Ngobeni Nghetlenge Case was born and bred at Joppie Village, N'wamitwa Tribal Authority, at Greater Tzaneen Municipality, Limpopo Province in the Republic of South Africa.

He is the first-born child in the family of seven, namely: Idah Tshameleni, Irene Rhabela, Madala Citizen, Harry Happy, Mashangu Webster, Hitekani Caroline. His father was a migrant labourer at Johannesburg, and he passed on in 1984 when Case was doing standard seven. His mother had to bring her offspring up single-handedly. She also passed on in 2005.

Mr. Ngobeni grew up like any other village boy. He started schooling at Mavhavaza primary school in 1976, and completed his Standard five in 1982 at the same school. He then proceeded to then Vasasele Secondary School in 1983, and later in 1988 he went to Bankuna Secondary School to do his Standard ten.

In 1989, he proceeded to the then University of the North (now University of Limpopo) to study for his BA (ED), which he completed within the prescribed period.

He started working at Vasasele High School in 1993, teaching learners Geography as a subject. He has enrolled in various universities, to further his studies.

Mr. Ngobeni is married to Tirhani Sandra Khosa. They have added four known offspring (at the time of writing this book) to the population.

He holds: B.A. (ED) University of the North, B. Ed (Hons), University of Pretoria, AMDP National School of Government.

He is the Assistant Director for Governance, attached to Nkowankowa Circuit, Department of Education. In July 2015, he was requested by the South African Broadcasting Corporation (SABC) to motivate listeners in the program called Gingirikani which is hosted by Khensani Myango.

He is a praise singer of Hosi N'wamitwa II.

In December, 2016, he has produced his first book titled The Heat of Your Silence, with the same publisher, William Jenkins.

His contact details: e-mail: **casengobeni@yahoo.com**

Cell no.: 0825418751 /0829540223

website: www.casengobeni.co.za

Foreword

It is said that man can live about forty days without food, about three days without water, about eight minutes without air, but only for one second without hope. Hope is the anchor of man's soul, without which many have given up on their dreams, on themselves, on others and even on God.

I would like to congratulate the author for taking the time to put hope filled words into this book, and for believing in the power of words to inspire hope. I had the opportunity of having the author stand-in for me on speaking engagements, and attest to the fact that his public speaking has inspired many lives. I am more excited about the book because it will reach much further and across generations. His hard work and selfless quest for brightening up the souls of people is evident in this book. This book is a great effort at investing in people which comes with great fulfilment and untold rewards, and this I speak from my personal experience as a Pastor.

Let me also congratulate you the reader and encourage you to invest in yourself. Your life is all you have and need for success. Success is locked inside every person waiting to be revealed. Only those who discover this truth and believe in their inherent God given potential succeed. Your soul was designed for success, it needs faith, hope and love for its good health, wealth and prosperity. As you read through the pages of this book, let it inspire you into your journey of self-discovery. External motivation is temporary; however, its power lies in its ability to help you discover your inner treasures that will energise you for life.

Pastor Strike Manganyi

Manna Tabernacle of Witness

20 November 2017

Acknowledgements

I would like to take my hat off to the following scholars, thinkers, philosophers, prophets, statesmen, priests, educators, martyrs, men and women, for having supported me and always motivated me to free my untapped potential. To those to whom I love, you know who you are.

- To all my siblings and offspring: I love you and I wish you the best of everything you ever wanted in life. You are part of my life and when you are away, I miss you dearly. I may not always stay in touch, but I care about you very much. I will love you until the Last Post. Partake and be patient.
- William Jenkins: (My publisher from Canada) I am speechless for the wonderful interest you always display to me, from my first book, The Heat of Your Silence.
- Mr Seabela Matome Jack (My father by choice, former teacher turned friend): Ordinary people think merely of spending time. Great people think of using it.
- Mr Mkhawana Hlupheka Solomon (My former teacher): It is better to have lived one day as a tiger than a thousand years as a sheep.
- Mr Makhubele Samuel Zambezi (My former teacher): Diamond does not lose its value due to lack of admiration.

- Mr Ngobeni Machoni Philpot (Brother): Our prime purpose in this life is to help others to achieve what they want.
- Mr Mhlongo Snider (Apostle): The same boiling water that softens the potato hardens the egg. It's about what you're made of, not the circumstances.
- Mrs Modika Pulane Philippine (Mopani District Manager Dept. of Education): If God brings you to it, He will surely bring you through it.
- Dr Mafenya LL (Mopani District Director, Dept. of Education): Only those who care about their work can hear you when you are quiet.
- Ms Nyango Agreement Khensani (Presenter Munghana Lonene FM): You are always one's favourite hello, and one's hardest goodbye.
- Mrs Maphophe Ruth (Executive Producer, MLFM): Quiet people have the loudest minds.
- Mrs Manzini Shalati Doreen (Circuit Manager, Dept. of Education): Life is like a mountain, hard to climb, but once you get to the top the view is beautiful.
- Pastor Manganyi Strike (Presenter Munghana Lonene FM): When everything seems to be going against you, remember that the airplane takes off against the wind, not with it.

- Bishop Malungana Mlunghisi Erasmus (Don't Blame God International Ministry): God sometimes takes us into troubled waters not to drown us, but to cleanse us.
- Mrs Joya Varhaghese (Director of St George College): Our greatest glory is not in never falling, but in rising every time we fall.
- Dr Baloyi Hellen (Mopani Manager Dept. of Education): Your smile, laughter, motivation, courage and inspiration are the best medicine and offerings you always give to us.
- Mr Nkuna Julius (Retired school principal): Everyone can buy a car, but not everyone can buy wisdom. Genius is eternal patience.
- Mr Marhanele Max Makisi (Prolific author): We are the sum total of what we have learned from all who have taught us, both great and small.
- Colleagues in the Department of Basic Education and my kith and kin: I'm nothing without you. There is no "I" without "us", and there is no "we" without our common humanity. *Munhu i munhu hi van'wana vanhu.* I am because we are, and I can only be a person through others. (RJ Khoza: Attuned Leadership).
- Mr Shikweni David (Colleague, friend and brother): Talent is a gift, but character is a choice.

- Hosi N'wamitwa II: As we sail through rough waters, we cannot avoid the storm. Calm seas never make skilful sailors. We can do anything, but we can't do everything.
- Mrs Mthembi Gavaza Tryphina (Friend and former classmate): David would not have been known had it not been for Goliath.
- Mr Manase Abram (Friend and former classmate, now based in USA): A champion is not necessarily a champion in the ring, he is only recognized there.
- Mr Nkuna Gezani Ezekiel (Former colleague at Vasasele High School): I have adopted your aphorism; an angry person cannot be a better judge.
- Let us all learn a good lesson from an eagle. The eagle does not fight the snake on the ground. It picks it up into the sky, changes the battleground, and then releases the snake into the sky.
- The snake has no stamina, no power and no balance in the air. It is useless, weak and vulnerable unlike on the ground where it is powerful, wise and deadly.
- Take your fight into the spiritual realm by praying and when you are in the spiritual realm, God takes over your battles.

- Don’t fight the enemy in his comfort zone. Change the battleground as the eagle does and let God take charge through your prayer.

Dedication

This book is dedicated to both paternal and maternal relations.

To my mother's family, the Mathevula family, I salute you and say:

Eka n'wina mhani wa hina,
Wena Tsakani Maggie,
Maggie wa Maxegani,
Maxegani wa Shivandzi,
Shivandzi wa Mpenyisi,
Mpenyisi wa Nkovani,
Nkovani wa Mujekejwa,
Mujekejwa wa Masuluke,
Masuluke -rithlavile-va – lwa-vurhena,
Hi mina Magogo,
Ndzi Xigogwana mina,
Ndzi gogile,
Hi mina Xivandzi xa timongo,
Xivandzi xa timongo ta nkanyi, ku huma tinxoxolombha,
Enyimpini ndzi vitana Magogo a tata goga,
Hi mina Nkovana mina,
I mani a nga tlulaka nkova loko wu tele hi mati?
I Mathevula ntsena hikuva wa delela,
Hi vadyi va timongo na swipamu hina,

Delayed Gratification

Hi vadyi va timphurugwa na tinchiri,
Hi hina va –ka-ehenhla ku ni ndlela,
Ha tlula loko nkova wu tele hi mati,
Murhi hi khandzinya hi nsinya hi chika hi rhavi,
Hi mina Madyela-Henhla,
Ku suka eka murhi wun'wana hi tlula kunene hi jitama eka lowun'wana murhi,
I Nghoni xilo xexo, xa chavisa,
Hi mina Xigidi!
Xigidi Xo gida vusiku xi gidela tintombhi to hlamba hi masi!
Hi mina Mantseku-ntseku!
Hi mina Marhendzeleka navo, kwala kusuhi nkarhi wa ha pfumela!
Hi mina Mabakanya va ha xuxa nkarhi wa ha ri kona!
Hi mina ncila a va ololi,
Wu olola hi wansati ntsena endzeni ka yindlu,
Hi mina tlutlama hi tamba,
Ndzi mbhurhi ya ribye mina,
Murhandziwana, lowo rhandziwa, Mundhondholovhani,
I Nghoni a nga dlhi'nkuku,
N'goba inkuku ya dlha inhlaza,
Inhlaza ya dlha imzimbha ka Nghunghunyane,
uNghunghunyane be kuyi nkosi ya Mashangani,

Delayed Gratification

Mina ngi Nkuzi ye 'Shangane mpela,
Hi mina loyi ndzi nga tsandza vavanuna hi magoza ensin'wini ya mavele!
Mina muheti-nkulu wa mavele ya vanhu!
Emasin'wini ya ntlhanu na manharhu!
Evuxeni va ndzi vitana N'wa-Tindzimi,
Evupeladyambu va ndzi vita Mulodwi, Mbulwa –ya - ku-fuma,
Edzongeni va ndzi vitana Khalanga!
En'walungu va ndzi vitana Munyayi-ku-Pinda!

I Mbhalati Vuputsu!
I Khoma na Ndzawu na Nghonyama!
I Xiaka na mirhi hi ku pfumala vo aka navo!
I Cucululu, wa marhaku ya ku chava ku tshama ehansi, ya chava ku singita vanhu!
Hi hina lavo huma eMusapa, eVunyayiri, Munyayi-ku-Pinda,
Lavo huma emaribyeni hi soko ra Gwambe,
Hi hina vakandzi va vutsulu eGombeni,
Hi hina va ka Xizula hi mirhi, Malwa-Ndlopfu,
Hi hina va ka rifu ra nhlikanhi,
A hi dlayiwi hi munhu hina,
Hi tifela hi hexe,
Va ka Tsumberi wa rifu enengeni,
Vahlangula va phosa ku fa,

Delayed Gratification

Matlula-ntsandza va yela vurhena,
Hi hina Maheta-byanyi- hi-ku-kasa,
I Ngungungu wa Xihlomulo,
Wa Gulukhulu –wa-Nchangameri,
Maleha-nyonga ya ka Valoyi,
Hi hina va ka xifun'wana, mahlakula hi rinhi ra nxolwana, a tshika xikomu
Hi hina va ka Gutse, va ka tinanga a ti rili, ku rila Mapalapala,
Xihlobyana lexi nga tala hi vulombe,
Kwale mahlanganini ya Rimbelule na Mithi, eHlavathini, eka Ndhambi,
Va ka ncila a va ololi, hi ncina mfenhe!
Hi hina va ka tshuri ra ngoma,
Hi hina va ka xindzhekwana xo ka byalwa xi ka ni vuputsu, xa le vuxakalandzanini bya le vutshudyanini,
Hi hina Malimbhandhu,
Hi mina Ximbhukutsu, mina gutsu ra mananga ra mapalapala,
Hi mina xivhoro-vhoro xa ku tambela na vakon'wana,
Laha xi taka hi kona ku sala ku nunwha ku ku mbveee!!!
Thevuya!
Nghoni!

Delayed Gratification

Mundhondholovhani!
Ximbhulukutsu!!
Khalanga!
Munyayi!
Mulodwi!
Baloyi!
Mongwe!
Mukansi!
Khalanga!
Mulodwi!
Mungoni!
N'wamitwa!
Nhlengani!
Xitsavi!

Delayed Gratification

To my father's, Ngoveni family to you I say:

Eka n'wina bava wa hina,
Wena Xinghalani Buraweni,
Nghala ya mona, mathlavela ku tshika,
Whe Nghala a xi hundzi tshanga xi nga yi tovatovangi,
Buraweni wa Pikinini,
Pikinini wa N'wamarhanga,
N'wamarhanga wa Xinghalani,
Xinghalani wa Masavani,
Masavani wa Machoni,
Machoni wa Xingurutela,
Xingurutela wa Masingiri,
Masingiri wa Ndzhavari,
Ndzhavari wa Mahohlo,
Mahohlo wa Hedeni,
Hi mina Ngoveni,
I Mulambya- ku- nyela,
Wo nyela' ndleleni a tshemba nkanu!
I masiya- a- govile, a govela vurhena!
I man'in'ina marilela nhonga,
I Makhwita- nhlaveni- mutwa -a- ri -na- wo' -nengeni!
I khwembe -ra- ndlala- xivupfa- hi- moya!
I Tshikisani wa miroho a xeva hi nyama,

Delayed Gratification

I Mahala-njhonjho-ka-pewula-inkomo -yi- fa- nga-mafutha!

Whe Nkuzi Madodeni,

Whe Nkuzi aba'y thandi y' thanda nga manqeba,
Whe Xikundzu-xa-mondzo lexi nga tsandza vavasati ku xi pandzela, xi kota hi ndzilo wa vuxika, ntsena!
Hi hina lavo tsandza hi ku xurha, ku dya ka vava, ku nya ka vava!
Hi hina va ka mbolo (nkava)-nkulu ya ka makhajani!

Laduma izulu!!!

Laduma libalele!

Isizwe a yi davuki ku davuka elizwe,

Ithambo lenyok'elihlaba elimzondayo ikhamba liyahleka lihleka na matombozana lithi khakhaaa!!!

Hi hina va ka xilwa –na- madzana, toya ri lwa -na-mayeka!

Matoya ya lwa na khume, tinhenha ti lwa na madzana-dzana!

I Xilobya-lobya, ka hlonge yi tlela exitikweni mundzuku va ta pfuka va vandzeka!

I Mphavava!!!

I Dzundzule N'walungu!

Keree, hi xinkobyana, famba hi ndhandha wa wena na mina ndzi ta famba hi wa mina!

I Njhenjhe matsakela mumu!

Isibongo sinhle sok'thambisa njhe nga mafutha!

Delayed Gratification

I phongololo masetheni, makitimela go ngwatha-
khope a ena mosadi!

I Bvewurisa hi Xikwembu!

I Kelengwani, mabolongwani,

Hi hina va ka hlakula hi rinhi a tshika xikomu,
nkonya wa sangu ekaya enchangana, evurila
nhlalala!

Hi hina va ka xivenga hi valoyi!

Loyi wo saseka hambi a etlele, a etlelele makumu
loyi!

I Ndwandwe, nwana wa Nghunghunyane, u
Nghunghunyani wa nghunghunya abafazi na
madoda ka Mandlakazi!

Hi hina va ka rifu ra nhlikanhi,

Hina a hi dlayiwi hi munhu hi tifela hi hexe,

Hi hina va ka xibabeni,

Ndwandwe ang'qokeli'endlin-inzingobo, zakhe u
qokela ephandle, ngob'izingub' zakhe zi na mafutha!

Hi hina va ka:

Masingiri,

Voyama,

Gumani,

Nkombyana,

Khubu,

Xikwakwa,

Xithlangoma,

Delayed Gratification

Xitari,
Xibotani,
Xinyangani,
Ncenye,
Ntlarhu,
Ntsemani,
Masiya.
Valambya!
Ndwandwe wethu!!
Valambya!
Ndwandwe wethu!

Chapter 1 Food for Thought

The Longer You Hold It, the Heavier the Weight

A psychologist walked around a class while teaching about problems to an audience.

As she raised the glass of water, everyone expected they'd be asked the "half empty or half full questions." Instead, with a smile on her face, she inquired: "How heavy do you think is this glass of water?" Answers called out ranged from 100g to 300g.

She replied: "The absolute weight doesn't matter. It depends on how long I hold it. If I hold it for a minute, it's not a problem. If I hold it for an hour, I'll have an ache in my arm. If I hold it for a day my arm will feel numb and paralyzed. In each case, the weight of the glass doesn't change, but the longer you hold it, the heavier it becomes."

Moral Lesson

The stress and worries in our lives are like that glass of water. Think about your problems for a while, nothing happens, but think about them a bit longer and they begin to hurt you. If you think about them all day long, you will feel paralyzed-incapable of doing anything.

It's important to remember to let go of your stress as early in the evening as you can; put all your burdens down. Don't carry them through the evening and into the night. Remember to put the glass down.

It doesn't matter who hurt you or broke you down. What matters is who made you smile again. Count your good deeds every morning and fill your mind with positive thoughts.

Be strong, but not rude. Be kind, but not weak. Be humble, but not timid. Be proud, but not arrogant. Break away from everything that stands in the way of what you hope to accomplish with your life.

If a rose smells better than cabbage, it doesn't mean the rose can make a better stew. Don't try to compare yourself too much with others. You have your own strength; find it and build on it. You make a better stew than they think. Smile always. All animals that exist were in the Biblical Noah's Ark. A snail is one of those animals. If God could wait long enough for snails to enter Noah's Ark, His door of grace won't close until you reach your expected position in life. Never look down on yourself; keep looking up. Broken crayons still colour.

"People don't care about what you say, they care about what you build." Mark Zuckerberg.

Coffee or a Cup?

A group of prestigious university graduates visited their old professor one day.

During the visit, the conversation turned to be at work: Graduates were complaining about countless difficulties and problems of life.

After offering coffee to his guests, the professor went to the kitchen and came back with a coffee pot and a tray, crowded with many different cups: Porcelain, glass, plastic and crystalline. Some cups were simple, other ones were expensive.

When the graduates picked out the cups, the professor said: "Notice, how all the beautiful cups were picked out, and the simple and cheap ones were left. And although it seems normal for you, wanting only good things for yourself is the source of your problems and stress.

You need to understand, that the cup doesn't make the coffee better. Most of the time it's only more expensive, but sometimes it is hiding what we are drinking."

Moral Lesson

Actually, all what the students needed was a coffee, not the cup. But they consciously chose the best cups. They then looked to see what kinds of cups others picked.

Delayed Gratification

Life is the coffee. Your job, money, position and society are the cups. They are just instruments for maintaining life.

The type of cup doesn't determine the quality of life. Sometimes, by concentrating only on the cups, we forget to enjoy the taste of coffee.

The happiest people are not those who have better things in life, but those who enjoy life and make the most of what they have.

Consider the following W's before choosing your cup of coffee:

- Who you are is what makes you special. Do not change who you are.
- What lies ahead will always be a mystery. Do not be afraid to explore.
- When life pushes you over, try to push forward harder.
- Where there are choices in life to make, make the ones you won't regret.
- Why things happen will never be certain. Take strides and move forward.

Happiness keeps you sweet, trials keep you strong, sorrows keep you human, failures keep you humble and success keeps you growing. Don't worry about the nature and the type of your cup, because the most important thing is the coffee - your life.

Delayed Gratification

We are well as individuals, but we become better when we blend with the right people. Coffee didn't know that it would taste nice and sweet before it met sugar and milk. The world is full of nice people. If you can't find one, be one yourself.

The richest wealth is wisdom. The strongest weapon is patience and memory. The best security is faith. The greatest tonic is laughter, and the greatest toxin is anger. The greatest force in life is love.

You cannot add milk to a cup full of milk, but you can still add sugar. Sweet people can always make their space, even in a filled heart or a cup full of milk. Add value, not ego.

Never change your originality for the sake of others because no one can play your role better than you. So, be yourself. You are the best. People respect the cups more than the tea.

Please don't be misled: People respect your position not you. They respect your position as their manager. You can resign today from that position, and see what will happen when you meet your former colleagues. You will be shocked to death!

When you are happy, you enjoy the music, but when you are sad, you understand the lyrics. One of the hardest decisions you'll ever face in life is choosing whether to walk away or to try harder. Don't walk away, try harder.

"Don't worry about people who don't worry about you at all!" Anonymous.

Stinking Tomatoes

A teacher asked her students to bring some tomatoes in a plastic bag to school. Each tomato was to be given the name of a person whom that child hates. The number of tomatoes would be equal to the number of persons they hate.

On a pre-determined day, all the children brought their bag of well-labelled tomatoes.

Some had two, some had three and some had five, some even had twenty tomatoes in accordance with the number of people they hated.

The teacher then told them that they had to carry the tomatoes with them everywhere they went for two weeks.

As the days passed the children started to complain about the decay and the smell of the tomatoes.

The students who had many tomatoes complained that the bag was very heavy to carry and the smell was too much and unbearable.

After a week, the teacher asked the students: "How did you feel this week?"

The students complained of the awful smell and heavy weight of the tomatoes, especially those who carried several tomatoes.

Moral Lesson

The teacher said: "This is very similar to what you carry in your heart when you don't like some people.

Hatred makes the heart unhealthy and you carry that hatred everywhere.

If you can't bear the smell of your spoilt tomatoes for a week, imagine the impact of bitterness in your heart as you carry it daily.

The heart is a beautiful garden that needs regular cleaning of unwanted weeds.

Forgive those who angered you. This makes room for storing good things. Strive to get better and not bitter. Try to cleanse your heart.

This is what happens in our daily lives. We always carry bags which are full of stinking tomatoes. Let us learn from these learners. They threw out the stinking bags of tomatoes and the hatred they represented..

Delayed Gratification

Sometimes you will create enemies as you live, and sometimes people will be your enemies for reasons best known to them.

Hate no one, no matter how much they have wronged you. Live humbly, no matter how wealthy you become. Think positively, no matter how hard life gets.

Give much, even if you've been given little. Forgive all, especially yourself. Never stop praying for the best for everyone.

Don't give your enemies a taste of their medicine. They already know how it tastes. Give them a taste of your own medicine.

If they lied, let your medicine be honesty. If they have played with your emotions, let your medicine be maturity. If they broke you, let your medicine heal. If they made you cry, let your medicine make them smile. Always stay true to yourself.

Remember, It is better for people to value you for who you are, not for who you pretend to be. Who you are lasts a lifetime, but who you pretend to be changes with the seasons, weather and climate.

Don't be afraid to be yourself, even if it means removing yourself from the life that you want to be in. You are, no doubt, worthy of being valued for who you are, so be who you are.

Nobody has ever gone up by bringing others down and no one has ever crossed to the other side by cutting others to pieces.

Your upward mobility depends on your behaviour towards others. You can never use rumours, gossip and lies to achieve your purpose. Always be aware of people who sweet talk you by assassinating other people's characters in your presence.

The same saw they use to cut others in your presence will be used to cut you into pieces in your absence. Be careful.

Life is like a coin. Pleasure and pain are the two sides. Only one side is visible at a time, but remember, the other side is waiting for its turn.

"Mathematics may not teach us how to add or how to subtract sadness. But, it does teach us one important thing: Every problem has a solution!" Anonymous.

My Time Will Come

An elephant and a dog became pregnant at the same time. Three months later the dog gave birth to six puppies. Six months later the dog was pregnant again, nine months on, it gave birth to another half-dozen puppies. The pattern continued.

Delayed Gratification

On the eighteenth month, the dog approached the elephant, questioning it about its pregnancy and said: "Are you sure that you are pregnant? We became pregnant on the same date, I have given birth to a dozen puppies and they are now grown to become big dogs, yet you are still pregnant!"

The elephant replied: "There is something I want you to understand. What I am carrying in my stomach is not a puppy, but an elephant. I only give birth to one elephant in two years. When my baby hits the ground, the whole earth feels it. When my baby crosses the road, human beings stop and watch in admiration. What I am carrying draws attention. It is mighty and great!"

Moral Lesson

Don't lose hope and faith when you see others receive answers to their prayers in a very short space of time. If you have not received your own blessings, don't despair, just say to yourself: "My time is coming. My blessings are being processed, prepared, packaged, and wrapped up in God's glory."

Never waste your time trying to explain who you are to people who are committed to misunderstanding you. They have already judged you. Don't waste your time with explanations. People hear only what they want to hear.

Delayed Gratification

Remember, Mother Nature always applies all her rules all the time.

Life and time are the best two teachers. Life teaches us to make good use of time and time teaches us the value of life.

We have to experience the bad times to be able to really appreciate the good ones. Just keep the faith; life will get better. When all else fails, learn from experience and move on. The world must move forward and it will do so with or without you.

A bond is not formed by the amount of time two people spend together, but rather by the experiences that are shared together.

If you can learn from worst times of your life, you will be ready to go into the best times of your life. Trying times are not the times to stop trying. One thing for sure is that truth is like the sun. You can shut it out for a time, but it isn't going away. We all want our lives to be simple and easy. We are always reaching, searching and finding out who we are until it is our time to leave this world.

Silence and a smile are two powerful tools that can be used to solve many problems. Sometimes the best way to solve some of the problems is to be silent. When you smile, you avoid hurting yourself.

If you let a person talk long enough, you'll hear their true intentions! Listen twice, speak once.

Try to speak only when you feel that your words are better than your silence.

"Remember, what we see determines what we do, and what we do determines the results." Steven R Covey.

Everyone has his Time Zone here on earth. Just because South Africa is one hour ahead of Nigeria does not mean that Nigeria is slow and South Africa is fast in doing its things. Both countries are operating in their own Time Zone.

Someone is still single, another got married and waited ten years before having a child, another had a baby within a year of marriage.

Someone graduated at the age of twenty-two, yet waited for five years before securing a good job. Another who graduated at twenty-seven secured employment immediately.

Someone became the principal of a school at the age of thirty and died at the age of fifty, while another became the principal of a school at the age of fifty and died at the age of ninety. Everyone follows a personal Time Zone.

Delayed Gratification

Everyone in this world is running their own race in their own lane and at their own pace. Time is the difference. Former president of USA, Barack Obama retired at the age of 55 as president, and Donald Trump began his presidency at age 70.

Your colleagues, friends and younger ones might seem to go ahead of you. Don't envy them or mock them. It's their Time Zone. You are in yours!

Hold on, be strong and stay true to yourself. All things will work together for your good. You are neither late nor early. You are very much on time.

"We don't develop courage by being happy every day. We develop it by surviving difficult times and challenging adversity." Barbara De Angelis.

The Dark Spots

One day a professor asked his students to prepare for a surprise test. He handed out the question paper, with the text facing down as usual. After handing it to his students, he ordered them to turn the page and begin writing. To everyone's surprise, there were no questions, just a small black dot in the centre of the page.

The professor then said: "I want you to write what you see there!"

The students got confused about this inexplicable task. At the end of the class, the professor read each one of them aloud in front of all the students.

All of them with no exceptions described the black dot, trying to explain its position in the middle of the page. After all, had been read the classroom was silent.

The professor began to explain. He said: “I am not going to grade you for this work. I just wanted to give you something to think about. No one wrote about the white part of the paper. Everyone focused on the black dot and the same happens in our lives. We always focus on the dark spots.”

Moral Lesson

The dark spots are very small things compared to everything that we have in our lives, but they are the ones that pollute our minds. Take your eyes away from the black spots in someone’s life and also in your life.

Enjoy each one of your blessings; each moment that life gives you. Be happy and live life positively.

No matter what you do, people will always try to build you up or break you down and it all depends on you permitting it. We learn something from everyone who passes through our lives.

Delayed Gratification

Some lessons are painful, some are painless, but all of them are priceless. The world could be a lot better if people would correct their own mistakes first, rather than criticizing one black spot.

Don't be upset with people and situations in your life because both are powerless without your reaction. You will always have people on your side if you let them know where you stand. Try not to take things personally. What people often say is a reflection of them and not you.

People will judge you because they don't feel good about themselves. Pain is optional and suffering is inevitable.

Our life is a gift given to us by God, with love and care and we always have reasons to celebrate.

However, if we insist on focusing only on the dark spots – health issues that bother us, the lack of money, complicated relationships with family members or the disappointment with a friend we are not living life to the full.

Life is like an elevator: On your way up, sometimes, you have to stop and let some people off. If people treat you as an option, leave them as a choice. Some people are like pictures. If you scale them too much, they lose their quality.

The world is full of nice people. If you can't find one, be one yourself. There is so much bad in the best of us and so much good in the worst of us. It is evil to find a dark spot in everything that you see. Try to look only for the best in every bad situation in which you find yourself.

Being a good person doesn't depend on your religion, status, life, race, skin colour, political views or culture. It depends on how you treat others.

Friendship is not about who acts true to your face. It's about people who remain true behind your back.

Faith isn't an emotion, it's a decision to walk a different road. When the storm comes, we keep on walking. The storm won't last; our faith will.

"Even if you dance on rain, your enemies will accuse you of raising dust." Anonymous.

Good Morning and Goodbye

There was a lady who worked at a meat distribution factory. One day when she finished with her work schedule, she went into the meat cold room (freezer) to inspect something, but in the moment of misfortune, the door closed and she was locked inside with no help in sight.

Although she screamed and knocked with all her might, her cries went unheard. Most of the workers had already gone and outside the cold room it was impossible to hear what was going on inside.

Five hours later, whilst she was on the verge of her death, the security guard of the factory opened the door. She was miraculously saved from dying of cold temperature that day.

When she later asked the security guard how he had come to open the door, which was not his usual work routine, he said: "I have been working in this factory for thirty-five years. Hundreds of workers come in and out every day, but you are the only one of the few who greet me in the morning and say goodbye to me every evening when you knock off. Many treat me as if I am invisible.

Today, as you reported for work, like all other days you greeted me in your simple manner by saying: 'Good morning'.

This evening after working hours, I curiously observed that I had not heard your 'Goodbye, see you tomorrow'. Hence, I decided to check around the factory. I look for your 'Hi' and 'Bye' everyday, because you always remind me that I am someone. By not hearing your 'farewell' today, I knew that something strange might have happened. That's why I was searching everywhere for you."

The lady cried hysterically and uncontrollably.

Delayed Gratification

Moral Lesson

Be humble, love and respect those around you. Try to have an impact on people who cross your path every day. You never know what tomorrow will bring, who will open the door of cold room (freezer) to you.

The only disability in life is bad behaviour. There comes a point in your life when you realize that everyone matters. There is no one who is the worst worm of the soil. Treat people the way you want to be treated. Talk to people the way you want to be addressed. Respect is earned not given.

People often judge you because they don't feel good about themselves. Don't be an option for anyone. Be a mandatory factor in their life. Remember, the earth revolves around the sun, not around you.

Morning wish is not a formality or a routine, it's the art of saying that: "I remember you on my first minute of the day and have a wonderful day, or I always think of you when I wake up, or I care a lot about you, or I love."

Your character is more important than your achievements. Achievements have importance only in the realm of time. Character is eternal. It determines our destiny. Don't be nice to people only when it's convenient to you. Genuinely nice people go out of their way to help others.

"Humble yourself, lest you be humbled. Learn from a banana tree, whenever it bears fruits; it bends down, because of the weight of the fruit. Do likewise and bend (bow) down. This is the symbol of humility." Maxwell Masakona.

Everything Went Well

A sixteen-year-old boy asked his mother: "Mom, what are you going to get me for my 18th birthday?" The mother answered: "Son, that's still a long way off."

The boy turned seventeen and one day he fell into a coma. His mom took him to the hospital where the doctor said: "Madam, your child has had a heart attack." His mom started crying. Coincidentally, on his 18th birthday, the boy recovered and was discharged from the hospital.

On his arrival home, he found a letter on his bed. The letter read: "My son, if you are reading this letter now, it's because everything went well. Do you remember the day you asked me what I was going to give you on your birthday? I didn't know what to say. I gave you my heart. Take care of it. Happy Birthday!"

The mother was dead because she had given up her heart to her ailing son.

Moral Lesson

Nothing is bigger than a mother's heart. That's why "mom" spelled upside down is "wow."

William Golding, British Novelist, Playwright and Poet, once asserted: "I think women are foolish to pretend they are equal to men. They are far superior and always have been. Whatever you give a woman, she will make greater.

If you give her sperm, she will give you a baby. If you give her a house, she will give you a home. If you give her groceries, she will give you a meal. If you give her a smile, she will give you her heart. She multiplies and enlarges what is given to her."

Nothing binds you except your thoughts, nothing limits you except your fear and nothing controls you except your beliefs. Everything is within you.

Good health does not always come from medicine. Most of the time, it comes from peace of mind, peace of health, peace of soul. It comes from laughter and love.

When a bowl is broken in your family, try to put back together the broken pieces with the cracks being filled with gold, creating a beautiful lining.

This is to emphasize the beauty in what was once broken.

Try to have a belief that when something has suffered damage and has a history, it makes it more beautiful. The same goes for human beings.

"Life is too ironic to fully understand it. It takes sadness to know what happiness is, noise to appreciate silence and absence to value presence." Anonymous.

The things that you've been through and are going through don't make your life uglier, although it may seem that way when you are going through them.

You are not broken beyond repair. Pick yourself up, learn from what has happened and become a better person because of the struggle that you've been through.

Nobody has ever had a perfect life and nobody ever will. Don't be ashamed of what has happened to you. Take up the broken pieces, merge them and paint them with gold.

There is a genuine reason for everything that has happened to you. Learn to accept and stop denying. If you are going through hard times, learn from it.

"Every next level of your life will demand a new you. Sometimes it takes being broken in order to become that new version of yourself." Anonymous.

Sinking Boat

A man was asked to paint a boat. He brought paint and brushes and began to paint. While painting, he realized that there was a hole in the boat and decided to repair it.

When he was finished painting, he received his money and left. The next day, the owner of the boat came to the painter and presented to him a nice cheque much higher than the payment of the painting.

The painter was surprised and asked: "You have already paid me for painting the boat!"

The owner of the boat responded: "This is not the payment for painting the boat. It's for having repaired the hole in the boat."

The painter replied:" Oh, but it was such a small service. Certainly, it's not worth paying me such a high amount for something so insignificant."

The owner: "My dear friend, you do not understand. When I asked you to paint the boat, I did not mention the hole. When the paint dried, my kids took it and went for a fishing trip.

They did not know that there was a hole in the boat. I was at home at that time. Imagine what went through my mind. When I saw them, I was relieved.

Then I found that the hole in the boat had been repaired by you. You saved me and my children. God, bless you!"

Moral Lesson

Repair the leak or a hole in someone's life. Wipe away tears and help others. Identify and appreciate those who repair the holes in your life, because those holes could have led to something big and disastrous.

Don't educate your children to be rich; educate them to be happy. So, when they grow up they will know the value of things not the price.

The owner of the boat and the person who was hired to repair it were real fathers who care about their children and jobs respectively.

A father is not defined as the man who makes children, but rather a man who extends his hands, time and heart to raise the children and gives his heart and love to his children.

Delayed Gratification

Genes do not always make you a father. Being a father comes from the heart. Any fool can make a baby, but it takes a man to raise a child.

Having God in your boat doesn't mean that you will not face any storm, but it means that no storm can sink your boat. Walk in faith and you will never walk alone.

Learning to love is less about perfection and more about progress. When you turn your worry into worship, God will turn your battles into blessings.

There are many people who we meet in our lives, but only a very few will make a lasting impression on our minds and hearts. It is these people who we will think of often and who will always remain important to us as true friends.

You will always be part of some people's life. You will never find where you fit, but others will fill up the empty spaces in their lives with pieces of you. Other people's lives may not be complete without you. Be a blessing to others and not a curse. Amen!

"Never love someone who treats you like you're ordinary." Oscar Wilde.

When Will My Fingers Grow Back?

While a father was polishing his new car, his six-year-old son picked up a stone and scratched lines on the side of the car.

In anger, the father took the child's hand and hit it many times. The son was then taken to the hospital where they amputated all his fingers due to multiple fractures.

When he realized that he has lost all his fingers, he painfully asked his father: "Dad, when will my fingers grow back?" His father was so hurt and speechless.

He went back to his car and kicked it a lot of times, devastated by his own actions. He looked at the scratches and he was shocked when he saw what was written by his fingerless son.

The child had written: "I love you, Dad!"

The next day, the father committed suicide.

Moral Lesson

Let us try to manage our anger, no matter what and how. Anger and love know no limits. Things are to be used and people are to be loved. In today's life, people are used and things are loved.

Watch your thoughts; they become words. Your words become your actions. Your actions become habits. Habits become character and your character becomes your destiny.

Love those who love you and forget those who don't value you. Sometimes the smallest act of love can take up the biggest space in someone's heart.

One day an eraser was talking to a pencil.

Pencil: I'm sorry, eraser.

Eraser: For what?

Pencil: I'm sorry you always get hurt because of me. Whenever I make a mistake, you're always there to erase it. As you make my mistake vanish, you lose a part of yourself and get smaller and smaller each time.

Eraser: That's true, but I don't really mind. You see, I was made to do this, I was made to help you whenever you do something wrong, even though one day I know I'll be gone. I'm actually happy with my job. So please, stop worrying, I will not be happy if I see you sad.

Reflection: Our parents are just like the eraser, and we are the pencil. They're always there for their children, cleaning up their mistakes. Sometimes along the way they get hurt and become smaller (older and eventually pass on).

Take care of your parents, treat them with kindness and most importantly, love them.

"Never reject anyone on account of their weakness, because the future is a mystery. If you reject them, you are also rejecting their strengths." TB Joshua, SCOAN.

Clapping of Hands Is Not Always Appreciation

A young mosquito went out flying on its first day.

When it returned home, the mother asked: "How was your first flying day, my dear?"

The young mosquito answered with joy and smile: "Every person I was flying on top of the head was clapping hands for me, others were ululating. It was a nice experience."

The mother with tears in her eyes responded: "Thank God, you came back alive. They were not clapping hands for you. You just escaped; they wanted to kill you."

Moral Lesson

Not everyone who claps hands for you is happy to see your success and not everyone who smiles and hugs you loves you.

Beware, some wish to see you going down, so, don't trust every smile and hug you get because they may want to kill you. Hatred can come from anyone, including your next of kin.

Parents should also inspire manners in their children as follows:

- When entering your house, greet your children with hugs and kisses. This should develop their sense of love and mercy.
- Be good to your neighbours and never backbite. Never speak ill of other drivers when on the road, because your children listen, absorb and emulate.
- When calling your parents, encourage your children to speak to them. When visiting your parents take your children with you. The more they see you take care of your parents the more they learn to take care of you.
- When driving them anywhere, don't always play music. Rather, tell them the stories yourself. This will have a greater impact on their lives.
- Read to them a short story and even a scripture a day. It doesn't take much time. It will create a strong bond and wonderful memories.
- Wear presentable clothes, even if sitting at home and not going out for a day. Your children need to learn that being clean and tidy has nothing to do with going out.

- Try not to blame or comment on every word or action they say or do. Learn to overlook and let go sometimes. This will certainly build their self-confidence.
- Ask your children's permission before entering their rooms. Don't just knock and enter, but wait for a verbal permission. They will learn to do the same when entering your room.
- Apologise to your children if you have made a mistake. Apologizing teaches them to be humble and polite.
- Don't be sarcastic or make fun of your children's views or feelings, even if you "didn't mean it" and was "only joking." It really hurts.
- Show respect to your children's privacy. It's important for their sense of value and self-esteem.
- Pray with them. Teach them how to pray. Lead by example.

"Surround yourself with people who bring out the best in you. Stop competing with people. A flower does not think of competing with the flower next to it. It just blooms." Anonymous.

The Struggles Are Part of Our Journey

A boy was playing outside his house when he saw a fascinating caterpillar. Every day, he would go to the caterpillar and bring some leaves as its food.

One day, the caterpillar climbed up on a small branch and started to transform into a cocoon. The boy watched every day, waiting for the cocoon to become a butterfly. One day a small hole appeared in the cocoon and the butterfly started to struggle to come out.

At first the boy was excited, but soon he became concerned. The butterfly was struggling so hard to come out! It looked like it couldn't break free! It looked desperate! It looked like it was making no progress at all.

The boy was so touched, and he decided to help. He ran to get a pair of scissors and then walked back.

As he was about to cut the cocoon, their scientist neighbour shouted as he passed by, and said: "Son, if I were you, I wouldn't do that." The boy was shocked and asked: "Why, uncle?"

The scientist neighbour responded: "The butterfly was supposed to struggle. In fact, its struggle will push it and make its wings very strong. The greater the struggle, the stronger and more beautiful its wings will become."

Moral Lesson

Just like the butterfly, the struggles are part of our journey and are preparing us for what awaits us. Sometimes it's painful, but these challenges hone our skills and make us strong in the end. Your struggles, setbacks, problems and other challenges are all necessary for your own development.

We may dodge our responsibilities, but we cannot dodge the consequences of dodging our responsibilities.

Remember, in the winter season, one hot day does not make a summer. It will still be winter. Never, I repeat, try to put something that God did not put in all the organs and parts of the human being. There is no omission. Every part knows its role and responsibilities.

Any factory fault will be fixed only by the Dealer-Maker!

There is a lesson of time-Karma which says: When a bird is alive, it eats ants. When the bird is dead, ants eat the bird. Time and circumstances may change at any time. Don't devalue or hurt anyone in life. If you do, apologise. You may be powerful today, but time is more powerful than you.

One tree makes a million match sticks. Only one match stick is needed to burn a million trees, so be good and do good.

Even your worst days have only 24 hours. You should stop fighting your battles with words; your battles should be fought on your knees!

Worries and tensions are like birds. We can't stop them from flying near us or above our heads, but we can certainly stop them from making a nest in our minds.

In his ***If you're not growing you are dying***, Dr David Molapo once advised: "No diamond or gem has ever been polished without friction. It is the irritation in the oyster that produces the pearl. The problems, difficulties and setbacks we have in life are all necessary for our own development."

The struggle you are in now is preparing you for more challenges and battles ahead.

Not all great people are powerful and contrary to that, not all powerful people are great!

"As we sail through rough waters, we cannot avoid storms. Calm seas do not make skilful sailors." Anonymous.

Happiness Cannot Be Deferred

One day a beautiful, expensively dressed, rich lady complained to her psychiatrist that she felt that her whole life was empty, it had no meaning. So, the lady went to visit a counsellor to seek happiness.

The counsellor called over the lady who was a cleaner of the office floors. The counsellor then said to the rich lady: "I'm going to ask Mary here how she found happiness. All that I want from you is to listen to her."

So, the lady put down her broom and sat on a chair and told her story. She said: "Well, my husband died of malaria and three months later my only son was killed by a car. I had nobody. I had nothing left. I couldn't sleep, I couldn't eat, I never smiled at anyone, I even thought of taking my own life.

Then one evening a little kitten followed me home from work. Somehow, I felt sorry for the kitten. It was cold outside, so I decided to let the kitten in. Then it purred and rubbed against my leg and, for the first time in months, I smiled. Then I stopped to think.

I asked myself many questions, because if a cat could make me smile, could I do something for people. Maybe doing something for people could make me happier.

So, the next day I baked some biscuits and took them to a neighbour who was sick in bed. Every day I tried to do something nice for someone. It made me happy to see them happy because of me.

Today I don't know anybody who sleeps and eats better than I do. I have found happiness by giving it to others."

When the rich lady heard this, she cried hysterically, just like a child. She had everything that money could buy, but she had lost the things which money cannot buy.

Moral Lesson

The beauty of life does not depend on how happy you are, but on how happy others can be because of you. In my first book, *The Heat of Your Silence,* I have reiterated the fact that there are many things that money cannot buy, like sleep, happiness, life, even blood.

Happiness is not a destination, it's a journey. Happiness is not tomorrow, it is now. Happiness cannot be deferred. Happiness is not dependency, it's a decision. Happiness is what you are, not what you have.

Be happy, enjoy every moment of your life. Life is too short to waste on grudges. Laugh when you can, apologise when you should, and let go of what you cannot change.

There is an African proverb that says: "Judge not your beauty by the number of people who look at you, but rather by the number of people who smile at you."

Holes in the Heart

There was a little boy who had a bad temper. His father gave a bag full of nails and told him that every time he lost his temper, he must hammer a nail into the back of the wall.

The first day the boy had driven thirty-seven nails into the wall. Over the next few weeks, as he learned to control his anger, the number of nails hammered daily gradually dwindled down.

He discovered that it was easier to hold his temper than to drive those nails into the wall.

Finally, the day came when the boy didn't lose his temper at all. He told his father about it and the father suggested that the boy now pull out one nail for each day he was able to hold his temper.

The days passed and the young boy was finally able to tell his father that the nails were all gone.

The father took his son by the hand and led him to the wall.

Delayed Gratification

Moral Lesson

The father said: “You have done well, my son, but look at the holes in the wall. The wall will no longer be the same again. When you say things in anger, they leave a scar, just like this one.

Once you hurt your loved ones, it won’t matter how many times you say ‘I am sorry’, the wound will still be there, because some wounds never heal, they just stop bleeding.

A verbal wound is as bad as a physical one. Remember: Good friends are rare jewels indeed. They make you smile and encourage you to succeed, they lend an ear, they share words of praise and they always want to open their hearts to us.

Nothing hurts more than being disappointed by the person you thought would never hurt you. It hurts the most when the person who made you feel special yesterday makes you feel so unwanted today. Don’t ask why someone keeps hurting you. Ask yourself why you’re allowing them.

Apologies don’t mean anything if you keep doing what you’re sorry for.

Sometimes, the person you’d take a bullet for ends up being the one behind the gun. Words hurt more than everything else can, because they last, sometimes forever.”

"A tongue has no bones but it's really strong enough to break a heart. It only takes a few seconds to hurt someone, but sometimes it takes years to repair the damage." Anonymous.

Seven Wonders of the World

A group of students were asked to list what they thought were the present "Seven Wonders of the World."

Though there were some disagreements, the following received the most votes:

- Egypt's Great Pyramid
- Taj Mahal
- Grand Canyon
- Panama Canal
- Empire State Building
- St Peter's Basilica
- China's Great Wall

While gathering the votes, the teacher noted that one student had not finished her paper yet. So, she asked the girl if she was having trouble with her list.

The girl replied: "Yes, a little. I couldn't quite make up my mind because there were so many."

The teacher said: “Well, tell us what you have and maybe we can help you.”

The girl hesitated, then she read: “The Seven Wonders of the World are as follows: To see, to hear, to touch, to taste, to feel, to laugh, to love and true friendship”.

The classroom was so quiet you could have heard a pin drop. Finally, to break the silence, the girl started crying at the top of her voice.

Moral Lesson

The things we always overlook as simple and ordinary and that we take for granted are truly wondrous.

A gentle reminder is that the most precious things in life cannot be built by hand or bought by man. All precious things are natural, cheap and free, like the oxygen in the air we breathe.

Friendship is also precious and free. A friend is one who knows you as you are, understands where you have been, accepts what you have become, and still gently, allows you to grow.

Forgiveness is the best form of love. It takes a strong person to say they're sorry and even stronger person to forgive. A friend is someone who knows all about you and loves you just the same.

Friendship is like standing on the wet cement. The longer you stay, the harder it is to leave. If you try to go, you can't go without leaving a footprint.

Best friends understand when you say: "Forgive and forget." Friendship isn't about who you have known the longest, but it's about who came and never left you alone when you needed someone the most.

The most wonderful places to be are not in the Seven Wonders of the World, but are being in someone's thoughts, in someone's prayers and in someone's heart.

Memory which lasts forever will never die, but lives forever. Stay with me and never say goodbye to me and I will also do the same because I love you. Ii is best when couples act like best friends and when best friends act like couples.

"Anger is the most impotent of passions. It affects nothing it touches. It hurts the one who is possessed by it more than the one against whom it is directed." Clarendon.

To the world you are just one person, but to the other person you may be the whole world. In any relationship and friendship, the first person to apologise is the braver and the first to forgive is the stronger and the first to forget is the happier. Does it make sense or no sense or nonsense?

I have always been afraid of losing the people I love, but sometimes I keep asking myself: Is there anyone who is afraid of losing me too?

None of us knows what might even happen in the next few seconds, yet we still go forward because we trust and we have faith in the Almighty. Amen!

A friend who understands your tears is much more valuable than many friends who know only your smile.

A strong relationship doesn't need a daily conversation. It doesn't need that you always be together. As long as the relationship lives in the heart, true friends will never part. When the rest of the world walks out of your life, a true friend walks into your life.

This touching line was said by me to my wife one day: "Darling, when I die, don't come near my corpse, because my hand may not be able to wipe your tears anymore."

True friendship is like a rose. We don't realise its beauty until it fades. Just being there for someone can sometimes bring hope when all seems to be hopeless. A friend gives hope when the morale is low.

Broken Bricks

There is a time when the builders start searching for broken bricks so that they can fill a gap to make their work complete.

Moral Lesson

Some of us are like broken bricks. We were ignored, thrown away, considered as people of no value to the world, but the time has come or is coming when there is a need of you to be filled into their projects or lives to make them complete.

At this point they cannot and will not do anything without you. Their projects will not look better if you are not included.

Whether you agree with me or not, the fact of the matter is that you are a solution to somebody and somebody's life will never be complete unless you are involved.

They may too proud today, ignoring your presence, expertise, qualifications and your efforts, but soon and very soon, you will be needed.

You are better than what you think you are. Stop looking down on yourself just because somebody said something that made you feel inferior. You are a product of grace. Your life will be rewritten soon.

You are an asset. Someone is looking for you. Someone, somewhere is praying to meet a person of your calibre.

Do not compare your life to others. There is no comparison between the sun and the moon. They all shine when it's their time.

"Don't be upset when people reject you. Nice things are rejected all the time by people who can't afford them." Anonymous.

Can You Define Yourself?

A rat swallowed a diamond and the owner of the diamond contracted a man to kill it.

When the rat hunter arrived to kill the rat, there were more than thousand rats bunched up and one sitting by itself away from the pack. He killed the one sitting by itself away from the pack, and that was that one that had swallowed the diamond.

The amazed owner of the diamond asked: "How did you know it was that rat?" He responded: "Very easily! When idiots get rich, they don't mix with others."

Moral Lesson

When God answers your long-awaited prayers, maintain your normal profile. Don't be too proud and brag about your resources.

Delayed Gratification

"P-r-i-d-e" is a five-letter word, but it can destroy a twelve-letter word, r-e-l-a-t-i-o-n-s-h-i-p." Some people who are born from a poor family background, have the tendency of isolating themselves from others when they become successful.

"Two things define you: your patience when you have nothing and your attitude when you have everything." Anonymous.

Reciprocity of Concern

A very poor man lived with his wife whose hair was very long. One day the wife asked her husband to buy her a comb for her long hair so that it can continue to grow well and be well groomed.

The husband felt sorry and said he didn't have money even to fix the strap of his watch which had just broken.

The wife did not insist.

On his way to work that day the husband passed by a watch shop, sold his damaged watch at a low price and went to buy a comb for his wife. He came back home in the evening with a comb in his hand ready to give it to his wife.

He was surprised to see his wife with very short hair. She had cut and sold her long hair and bought a brand-new watch for her husband.

Tears flowed simultaneously from their eyes, not for the futility of their actions, but for the reciprocity of their love.

Moral Lesson

Love is when the other person's happiness is more important than your own. Give love and show love where it matters. How great our world will be if only we, as a couple, friends, colleagues, neighbours outdo each other in love and sacrifice.

How awesome it will be that we always think of each other every day. Don't base your love on conditions.

"Love is not love which alters when it alteration finds or bends with the remover to remove." Shakespeare, Sonnet 116.

Delay Your Judgement

A maid was so faithful that the woman could leave her baby with her and go out to attend other matters. She always returned to find the child soundly asleep with the maid faithfully watching over her.

One day something tragic happened. As usual, the woman left the baby in the "hands" of the faithful maid and went out for shopping. When she returned, she discovered rather a nasty scene, there was a total mess.

The baby's cot was dismantled, his nappies and clothes torn to shreds with blood stains all over the bedroom where she left the child and the maid. Shocked, the woman wailed as she began looking for her baby.

All of a sudden, she saw the faithful maid asleep under the bed. The maid was in a pool of blood.

The woman went berserk and assumed that the maid had killed her baby. She then rushed to the car and took the gun and shot at the maid, killing her instantly.

She continued searching for the remains of her baby, and she beheld another scene. Close to the bed was the baby, who although lying bare on the floor, was safe. There was a body of a big snake under the bed.

The body of a snake was torn into pieces in what must have been a fierce battle between it and the maid who was now dead.

The reality dawned on the woman who now began to understand what took place in her absence. The maid fought to protect the baby from the ravenous snake.

It was too late for her now to make amends because in her impatience and anger, she had killed the faithful maid. She then took the maid to hospital, not knowing that she was dead. At the hospital, she was told that her maid was dead and there was nothing they could do. However, the post-mortem found that the maid had died of a bullet wound, despite the fact that there was venom of a snake in her blood.

Moral Lesson

How often have we misjudged people and torn them to shreds with harsh words and deeds before we have had time to evaluate the situation?

We presume things our way without taking the trouble to find out exactly what the situation really is. A little patience can drastically reduce major lifelong mistakes. Who are you misjudging now?

Be patient with people before you regret your actions against them. Be quick to hear but slow to respond and become angry.

No matter who you are, how experienced you are, or how knowledgeable you think you are, always delay judgement. Give others the privilege to explain themselves. What you see may not be the reality. Never conclude for others.

We should never focus only on the surface and judge others without understanding them first.

Those who like to pay the bill, do so not because they are loaded but because they value friendship above money. Those who take the initiative at work, do so not because they are stupid, but because they understand the concept of responsibility.

Let us learn to apologise, not because we are wrong and the next person is right, but because we value our relationship more than our fighting.

Those who are willing to help you, do so not because they owe you anything but because they see you as a true friend. Those who call you do so not because they have nothing to do, but because you are in their hearts and they also know the importance of keeping in touch.

"My dear brothers, take note of this: Everyone should be quick to listen, slow to speak and slow to become angry." James1:19 NIV

Chapter 2 Types of People

Little is known about the origin of the word, people. The common understanding is that *people* originates from the Anglo-French or old French meaning: "people, population, crowd, mankind, humanity," from Latin Populus "a person, nation, body of citizens, a multitude, crowd, throng," of unknown origin, possibly from Etruscan. The Latin word also is the source of Spanish Pueblo and Italian people. In English, it displaced native folk.

There are various types of people that give this beautiful universe its natural beauty and good aroma. They range from big and small, ugly and beautiful, weak and strong, givers and receivers.

The following are some of the types of people:

Horses with Blinkers

Blinkers are usually made of leather or plastic cups that are placed on either side of the eyes, either attached to a bridle or to an independent hood. Blinkers that have a peep hole cut in the back of the cup are known as visors.

Many racehorse trainers believe these keep horses focused on what is in front, encouraging them to pay attention to the race rather than other distractions, such as crowds. Additionally, blinkers are seen on driving horses, to keep them from being distracted or spooked, especially on crowded city streets.

Most equestrian disciplines, other than racing and harness competition, do not permit the use of blinkers at any time, under penalty of elimination. In racing, blinkers are usually seen attached to a synthetic hood placed under the bridle. In driving, they are attached to the bridle's cheek pieces.

Rationale of Horses with Blinkers on People

Some people are easily distracted by anything around them. The blinkers on a horse are put just along its long jaws towards its eyes. When it runs and realizes that there is another running alongside it, it stops immediately or changes its velocity.

These blinkers assist the horse a lot, because it prohibits it from seeing what is around it. Even when the crowd ululates, without these blinkers, the horse stops. Some people change their focus or plans overnight because someone said that they cannot attain or fulfil their dreams.

To put more insult to a wound, even when the crowd is supportive, to them means nothing. People are making a positive noise around you in order to encourage you to outrun the others in a race.

Remember, you are always the master of your own destination. Stay focussed, don't get distracted. Develop your own mission and vision statements.

Delayed Gratification

Nobody elsewhere in this world is living your own life. There two sets of people in your life. First is your family. They want to see you succeed and prosper in life. Second are those who are not your relatives. Some of them do not want to see you succeed in life.

Walking is the best exercise in life. Do not run; just walk. Learn to walk away from arguments that lead you to anger, hatred and vengeance. Positive arguments are healthy, however. They can build and develop you.

Stay away from situations and people who are always affecting your emotions. Some people can deliberately put you down and also despise you. Avoid them. Some thoughts sometimes reduce your worth.

You must remember that you are not born of a mistake. You are worth more than you can imagine and your potential is unlimited. You do not have to put on blinkers because you know where you are heading.

Do away with fear and failure that stifle your dreams. The number one enemy of any human being is fear and failure. There are people who also do not care for you and who are opportunistic. Walk away from this group also.

Some people are toxic. Why do you associate with them? Stay with people who love you unconditionally. Blinkers are for narrow minded people and not you. Watch out. Be with those who bring out the best in you, not those who increase the stress in you.

You are born of people who turned shame into triumph.

"No matter how many mistakes you make or how slow you progress, you are still way ahead of everyone who isn't trying." Tony Robinns

Revolving Door of People

A revolving door is the door that rotates. It rotates about a central vertical axis, especially with four leaves arranged at right angles to each other, thereby excluding draughts.

Rationale of Revolving Door of People

There are people who cannot take a firm decision in their lives, just like a revolving door, they rotate in one area. Literally, when they get inside the house through the revolving door, they meet some people who are coming out and instead of going to the home owner to help, they simply move out with those who are going out.

The pattern continues, when they get out they meet others who are getting in and they join them. The rotation goes just like that repeating itself.

These types of people move with people. They cannot decide on their own without consulting anyone, even when they want to eat, they first ask: “Am I hungry, my friend...? Is it cold, can I put on my jacket?” These people do what the mob or crowd is doing.

Take note of the following hints: Where you end up in life is not determined by where you start. It’s what you choose to do with the seconds you have; it is what you choose to do with your potential that shapes your destiny. You can choose to be selfish or to be selfless.

You can choose to make a difference in your life or another person’s life. I personally have learned that there are only two things that will create your dreams, first are your choices. If you want to rotate in a revolving door, the choice is yours.

Second, is your commitment to those choices. Your choices will either make or break you. Some choices will lead you to an amazing life. Try to be kind to everyone - even the ones that you feel that they do not deserve it. Always smile at the challenges, because there is a divine gift hidden in them.

Embrace change, because resisting it will only lead to frustration. Avoid finger-pointing as much as possible. Be in charge wherever you are.

Take responsibility. When you blame, you give your power away. Believe in your dreams; if you don't, nobody else will. Do not believe in people you meet in the revolving door. You are not sure why people on the revolving door are getting in or out.

Strive every day to become just a little bit better. People who saw you yesterday should see a new person today. Some people don't change. What you saw in him yesterday, is still the same even today. Soon you will be a master at what you do.

Do not let anyone steal your beautiful dreams because they are your greatest assets. Do people think of you when they have their own problems? Be part of the solution, not the problem.

The biggest problems you are willing to solve the bigger the rewards you will get. Even on the revolving door, open your heart to strangers; they are just friends you haven't met yet. Do what you fear and you will overcome it.

Push that revolving door. Get in and do what you want to do and get out.

"Choose to make a difference. Most people just choose to stay alive. Do not allow yourself to be influenced by negativity."

Constantly seek advice from people who have more experience, knowledge and success than you do. It will speed up your journey to success tremendously.

Avoid putting more focus on the past. It doesn't equal your future.

Always and always keep your word.

Choose to believe in yourself before you can believe in another person. You have the power to create and change anything.

Really, you can do it. Complain less and take more action. Don't accept mediocrity. Choose excellence. Nobody is born mediocre. It's a choice.

Forgive those who have hurt you in the revolving door and let it go. Forgiveness liberates enormous amounts of energy and creativity.

Stand up for yourself and your beliefs. Say something good to everyone every day. Remember, if you change with every critic, you will be moving in a revolving door. Take advice also from those who once failed in the same attempt as yours.

"Men are developed the same way gold is mined. Several tons of dirt must be moved to get an ounce of gold. But you don't go into the mine looking for dirt. You go in looking for the gold." John C Maxwell.

People as Chameleons

A chameleon is a slow-moving Old-World lizard with a large tail, long extensive tongue, protruding eyes that rotate independently, and a highly developed ability to change colour.

The Arab Proverb says that a chameleon does not leave one tree until he is sure of another. In fact, a chameleon has no true colour because it takes the colour of the environment, mainly for defence purposes against its enemies. Just like an owl, the bird of the night, its eyes rotate through 360 degrees.

Rationale for People as Chameleons

There are people who adjust themselves to fit into whatever happens to be cool at the moment. These people fit into the situation of that moment in terms of character, appearance, interest, opinions, and personalities. Sometimes in social circles they are referred to as "scenesters, try-too-hard or idiots."

They take the personality of the person they're with at the moment, and this is either done subconsciously or as a sad attempt to make people like you. A chameleon is a person who often makes expedient or facile changes in ideas or character, and is subject to quick or frequent changes especially in appearance.

As a human being, you should know your true colour. Don't try to please people at the expense of your integrity. I know that not all of us have integrity! What a tragedy!

"We must always take sides. Neutrality helps the oppressor, never the victim. Silence encourages the tormentor, never the tormented." Elie Wiesel

Some people are like chameleons, they adapt to your favourite colour so you'll like them, but eventually their true colours always show.

One friend of mine once gave me a leaflet, full of advice when I was doing my exit level in secondary school. The leaflet was unsigned. It helped me a lot to know who I'm supposed to be. It reads as follows:

"My son, I have decided to write you this letter as a guide when you become of age. Listen to me, digest my words, weigh them and sift them. Take what is good for you and use it. I am not infallible, but I promise you my experience will be a reservoir of wealth for you.

Fear God and respect man. Never fear anybody as that will enslave your soul. Love and respect your mother. Heed her voice. She brought you into this world and brought you up under difficult conditions.

She is a wise mother who will always safeguard your best interests. Like any other person, she has her mistakes. Accommodate them and be long suffering.

Never discuss your mother's faults with strangers. Honour her and you will find favour with God. If you must correct her do it wisely. Love your sister and be considerate. Be her pillar and advisor.

Do not be too protective, but do advise and leave room for her discretion.

Pray at least twice a day, in the morning when you wake up and in the evening when you go to bed. Read your Bible for in it there is life and wisdom.

Never be a religious fanatic. Examine every doctrine you come across. Respect truth, and never honour lies. At the same time, be careful how you tell your truth.

Never be a coward and yet never be too bold. Never put all your trust in man.

Always leave room for surprises and disappointments. Be politically aware. Know what is going on around you.

Do not involve yourself in politics while at school. Finish your education first. But I say, always be aware even during your school days. Never, I repeat, be an informer.

Better is a dry slice of bread than a thick slab of cheese dipped in the blood of your brethren. The employers of the informer have no respect for him. They don't trust him, because they know he is just as dangerous to them as he is to the people he informs about.

There are many ideologies in this world. If you must follow one, I advise you to stay away from racism and communism. Each is as wicked, ruthless and ungodly as the other. These are Siamese, if not identical twins of wickedness.

Racism has gone the way of all the wicked. Their end is as incurable and violent as their rule. The Biblical Pharaoh and Adolf Hitler are two good examples.

Do not be too subversive. Violence is very costly as the great nations have learned. If you find yourself in a violent situation, then use your discretion.

Never feel sorry for yourself. If you fall, stand up and start afresh. If tomorrow you should be ruler in the land of your birth, administer justice fairly and equally among all of them. 'Think of the next generation and not the next election. When talking never generalise. It is a serious mistake,' Dr Alan Paton once advised me.

My son, stay away from a married woman. She is her husband's sacred altar. Do not defile her.

Never delight in the number of virgins you may have deflowered, as that will count heavily against you in life. Delight in wickedness demoralises a man.

Keep away from harlots and homosexuals. Stay away from liquor. It destroys soul. Never render a girl pregnant. If you do, do not run away from your responsibility.

That at the same time, does not mean you should marry her if you feel she cannot be the right partner.

Always observe your girlfriend's mother as that is how your girlfriend will behave if she becomes your wife.

Admit your mistakes. Never go to the grave denying the wrongs you have done.

My son, keep and honour this script. This is your will. Share it with your sister. It will enrich your soul and give life to you."

"Every person is either a creator of fact, or a creature of circumstances. He either puts colour into his environment, or like a chameleon, takes colour from his

environment. Or to put it in another way: some people are thermometers. They conform completely to their environment - their behaviour is definitely determined from without. Other people are thermostats. Instead of allowing their environment to control them, they determine the environment." Myles Munroe.

People as Chained Dogs

These are dogs which are chained by their owners at home, because they are either vicious or thieves. Their owners are aware that if they can leave them loose they might end up in trouble.

Every time when they move, they move only the distance of the rope or chain. In other words, even if they are no longer chained, they cannot move beyond their specified distance.

When the chained dog sees other dogs, it runs and barks at them only to the end of the chain, even if the chain is no longer there.

Rationale for People as Chained Dogs

Some people's minds are chained. They cannot even change in situations that fits them. To be in a comfort zone is dangerous because you do not grow.

Delayed Gratification

Try to seek new adventures and greener pastures. Your potential is unlimited, but the question is: "Do you know what you're capable of?"

Our families and communities have played a very big role in your upbringing. Either they told you that you are the worst worm of the soil and useless or you're the cream of the family or community. All these aspects created the type of the person who you are today.

Some were told that they were very ugly, intelligent, handsome, beautiful or worst that they will die young.

Remember, you are not an extension of whomever; you are your own self. Just tell yourself that you are capable, intelligent and you can also instruct mountains to move.

Your family background should not determine your destiny in life, but it should redirect you. Furthermore, it does not matter where you come from; what matters is where you are going.

Keep on running and never stop dreaming big. How many times have others discouraged you, but at the end you have accomplished your goals through determination and perseverance. People want you to do what they can also do. Prove them wrong. Do more. Disappoint them. Keep on pushing.

There is no successful person on earth who has had an easy past. It was tough and it is even tougher now. It's up to you to decide whether or not you will let the negative words of others affect your attitude and behaviour.

"If you think education is expensive, wait until you see how much ignorance costs." Barack Obama.

A Tree Analogy

An American actor and a comedian who specializes in gospel genre, Taylor Perry talks of three kinds of people: Leaf, branch and roots people.

He uses a tree analogy. He says that he always thinks of people in his life, be it friends, family, employees and acquaintances, as falling under three categories.

The leaf people:

These people come into your life in a particular season, just as leaves in a tree do. Their main purpose is to protect you and to give you shade only. Do not depend on them because they are too weak. They depend on you for their survival.

When it is too cold, too hot or when the wind blows in your life, they're gone. You can't be angry with them; they are who they are. They are seasonal.

The branch people:

There are people who come into your life like branches of a tree. Although they are stronger than leaves, you have to very careful with them. They will stick around with you through most seasons.

When there is a storm in your life, one or two, it's possible that you can lose them. They break away when times get tough despite the fact that they are stronger than the leaves.

These people cannot handle too much weight. Again, you cannot be angry with them; they are who they are. They are periodical.

The roots people:

If you find people in your life who are like the roots of a tree, then you've found something special. Like the roots of a tree, they are hard to find, because they are not trying to be seen.

Their only responsibilities are to hold you up and help you to live a strong, happy and healthy life. If you thrive and succeed in life, they are happy. They stay low key. If you receive an awful storm, they hold you up.

Their job is to nourish you and to feed you, come what may. They don't want to be seen by people. They even don't want praise.

They feed you, water you and also take care of you. When you are happy, they celebrate with you. When you die, they die with you. Look at your life. How many leaves, branches and roots do you have? What role do you have in people's lives? Thank God for your roots! Stop spending time with the wrong people. Life is too short to spend time with people who suck the happiness out of you.

"If someone wants you in their lives, they will make room for you. You should not consistently force people into your life who don't value you. You should not fight for a spot or position."

Remember, it is not the people who stand by you when you're at your best, but those who stand by you when you're at your worst who are your true friends.

Don't try to be someone you're not. One of the greatest challenges in life is being yourself in a world that is trying to make you someone else. Someone will always be smarter, someone will always be younger, but they will never be you!

So, don't change so that people can like you. Be yourself and people will like the real you.

Don't hold onto the past thinking that there is nothing new. You cannot start the new chapter if you keep on re-reading the previous one. Don't be scared to make a mistake. Doing something and getting it wrong is ten times better than doing nothing.

Every success has a trail of failure behind it and every failure is leading towards success. You end up regretting things you did not do far more than the things you did.

Stop getting involved in a relationship for the wrong reasons. Relationships must be chosen wisely. It is better to be alone than to be with bad company.

There is no reason to rush. If something is meant to be, it will happen at the right time, with the right person for the best reason.

Don't reject new relationships because old ones did not work. In life, you will realise that there is purpose for everyone you meet. Some will test you, some will use you, some will teach you, but more importantly, some will bring out the best in you.

Stop compensating for things which are not there. Stop trying to compete with everyone else.

Don't worry about what others are doing better than you. Concentrate on breaking your own record every day. Success is a battle between you and yourself only. Stop concentrating on someone who overlooks your worth.

The greatest pleasure in life is doing what people say you cannot do. Remember, the smile on one's face doesn't mean that his life is perfect. It means he appreciates what he has and what God has blessed him with, and that is life.

"No one is sent by an accident to anyone. There is always a reason. Stay away from negative people. They have a problem for every solution."

Stay focused on your goals, your peace and your happiness. Don't waste time on anything that doesn't contribute to your growth.

Try to move fast in all your activities, because procrastination is a thief of time and life is short. Move enough and break things, if possible.

Unless you are breaking stuff, you are not moving fast enough. Successful people have two things on their lips: Silence and Smile.

Some people have been ironically buried alive. Those who buried them didn't know that they were burying a seed that would germinate one day and multiply itself.

Strive to have wisdom and not more money. Money is like the HIV/AIDS epidemic in that everyone says they don't have it even if they do have it.

One of the best gifts you can give someone is thanking them for being part of your life.

Be proud of your scars and that you're still standing. Every job is a self-portrait of the person who does it. Autograph your work with excellence.

Sometimes you don't need someone to complete you. You only need someone to accept you completely.

You can't just give up on something because the situation is not ideal. Great relationships aren't great because they have no problems. They're great because both people care enough about the other person to find a way to make it work. All relationships go through hell, real relationships get through it.

In life, you will realize that there is a purpose in meeting every person you meet or know. Never regret knowing someone. Good people will give you happiness, bad people will give you a lesson and the best people will give you memories. God doesn't bring the people we want, but the people we need.

There are many people that we meet in our lives, but only a few will make a lasting good impression on our minds and hearts. It is these people that we think of most often and who will always remain important to us as true friends.

"Some people are there to test you, some will use you, some will teach you, and some will bring the best in you. Trust in God and appreciate everyone he brings into your life. There comes a point when you have to realize that you'll never be good enough for some people. The question is: Is that your problem or theirs? "Anonymous.

Never put temporary people in the permanent place of your life; and don't be afraid of removing the wrong people from the right place. Be bold to take any decisions concerning your life. If they call it pride, tell them it is class.

You cannot go anywhere with negative people. Negative people are like cars without fuel and engines. You can sit in them, but they will never take you anywhere.

You can't change what you see until you learn from what you see.

Be careful who you open up to, because only a few people care. The rest just want to have something to gossip about.

Some people come into your life like a dark storming night and when the storm is over and the sun rises it becomes a beautiful day.

Make beautiful days in your lives by removing the "storms" in your life. Weak people revenge, strong people forgive, while intelligent people ignore.

"No matter the economy of the jungle, lions will never eat grass! Even if education is free, rat will never go to the same school with a cat!" Anonymous.

Friends and Enemies

Everyone qualifies for your love, but not all people you love qualify to know the secrets of your life because some cannot handle it and others cannot wait to trade your secret for personal gain.

The enemy that will destroy you, will not come with a sword but a smile. Learning to keep a friend's secret is not only about trust, but also destinies are at stake. Nothing can be more dangerous and painful than to share your secrets with your enemies thinking that they are your friends.

There are three categories of friends, namely: associates, comrades and confidents.

Associates:

They team up with you to achieve a common goal. Most of the time they compete for the same prize or goal with you. Be very careful with these people; they may push you down in order to win a prize.

Comrades:

They team up with you just to fight a common enemy. They will be gone once the enemy is defeated. You should not be worried when they leave; they were with you for a reason.

Confidents:

They walk with you no matter how hard it gets. You need to be grateful if you have one.

It is true that every effort is not converted into success, but it is equally true that success does not come without effort.

Be a good person, but don't waste time to prove it. Always be the same person, even in the midst of confusion and darkness. Avoid responding to anyone who always invites your emotions. The less you respond to negative people, the more peaceful your life will become.

You are responsible for your own happiness. If you expect others to make you happy, chances are you'll end up disappointed. I respect people who tell me the truth, no matter how hard it is.

Don't be a parrot in life, be an eagle. A parrot talks way too much but an eagle is silent and has the will power to touch the sky.

"Love your enemies, but if you want to make them mad, ignore them completely." John Mason.

Never apologise to others for their misunderstanding of who you are. Money is the worst discovery of human life, but it is the most trusted material to test human nature.

Standing alone doesn't mean I am alone. It means I am strong enough to handle my pressure all by myself. The world is full of monsters with friendly faces.

If you want to be happy do not dwell in the past, do not worry about the future, focus on living fully in the present. Don't be afraid to change. You may lose something good, but you may gain something better.

Overthinking is the biggest cause of unhappiness. Silence is better than nonsense. Never get too attached to someone, because attachment leads to expectations and expectations lead to suffering.

Delayed Gratification

Talking about our problems is our greatest addiction. Break the habit. Talk about your joys. Try to remember everything you have done well, all the battles you have won and all the fears you have overcome and conquered.

Accept life like a pair of walking legs. The foot forward has no pride and the foot behind has no shame. Both legs know that their situation will soon change.

"Whenever you find yourself doubting how far you can go, just remember how far you have come." Anonymous.

Chapter 3 Life

Appreciate what you have

Never let the things you want in life make you to forget the things you have, no matter how insignificant. Enjoy these little things you have, for one day you will look back and realize they were the big things. Life is beautiful.

The person who loves you is not always the person who sees you every day, but the person who looks for you every day. Where there is great love, there are always miracles.

Be Happy

Be happy, not because everything is good, but because you can see the good side of everything. When you wish good for others, good things come back to you, and when you wish them bad luck, bad luck comes back to you. This is an element of reciprocity, or a Law of Nature. Sometimes talking to your best friend is the only therapy you need.

It's not what you have but who you have in life that matters. Issues should be communicated in families and elsewhere. Without communication, there is no relationship. Without respect and love, life is tasteless. Without trust, there is no relationship. Having a soulmate is not always about love. You can find your soulmate in a friendship too.

Spend most of your time with your beloved ones, because one day when you will look in your album of memories, they won't be there anymore.

Sometimes all you really need is someone who will take care of your words, even if you are no more. Sometimes life is a struggle. Without struggle, there is no progress. Surround yourself with those on the same mission as you.

Be Positive

No matter how positive you may be, the Devil will send negativity on your way to see how positive you will stay. You may start to lose friends when you are genuine in your dreams.

Truly honest people don't have many friends, but they do have real friends. Life is too short; spend it with friends who make you laugh and feel loved. Don't be a beggar of love, but be a donor of love.

Beautiful people are not always good, but good people are always beautiful. If you love something, set it free. If it comes back it is yours and if not, it was not meant to be yours.

"Just because I laugh a lot doesn't mean my life is easy. Just because I have a smile on my face every day doesn't mean that

something is not bothering me. I just choose to move on, and not dwell on all the negatives in my life. Every new moment gives me the chance to renew a new. I choose to be that." Anonymous.

Success does not just come and find you, you have to go and find it. No matter how busy someone is, if they really care, they will really find time for you.

Don't worry about what people say behind your back. They are the people who are finding faults in your life, instead of fixing theirs.

People always think that the most painful thing in life is losing the one you value. The truth is, the most painful thing is losing yourself in the process of valuing someone too much and forgetting that you are also special. No one is more human than anyone else.

Simple formulae for a happy life: Never try to defeat anyone, just try to win everyone. Don't laugh at anyone, but laugh with everyone.

American psychiatrist and author, Theodore Isaac Rubin asserted: "Happiness does not come from doing easy work, but from the afterglow of satisfaction that comes after the achievement of a difficult task that demanded our best."

Life is a mirror, it will smile at you if you smile at it; if you frown, it will also frown. A bad attitude is like a flat tire. You can't go anywhere until you change it.

If you look at yourself in the mirror and you see an elephant, that is who you are, if you see an ant, that is also who you are. Think positively and you will create a positive image of yourself.

Make Good Choices

Life is determined by your choices. There are two things that can create your dreams: Your choices and your commitment to those choices. Your choices can either make you or break you. Believe in your dreams, if you don't nobody else will. Some of these choices should be as follows:

- Where you end up in life is not determined by where you started. It's what you choose to do with the time you have that matters. It's what you choose to do with the potential you have that shapes your destiny.
- You can choose to be selfish or you can choose to be selfless.
- You can choose to make a difference.
- You can choose to be kind to everyone, even to those who don't deserve it.
- You can smile at challenges as there is a divine gift hidden in them.

- You can embrace change. Resisting change will lead to frustration.
- You can choose to take responsibility for your actions. When you blame others, you give your power away.
- *"A relationship is like a bird. If you hold it tight, it dies. If you hold it loosely, it flies. But if you hold it with care it remains with you forever." Anonymous.*

Try to be better

- Strive every day to become just a little bit better. Soon you will be a master at what you do.
- Be part of the solution, not the problem. The bigger the problems you are willing to solve the bigger the rewards you will get.
- Open your heart to strangers. They are just friends you haven't gotten to know yet.
- Choose to make a difference. Most people just choose to stay alive instead of living.
- Try to make a difference in other people's lives.
- Ask why you want others to add value to your life. What are you doing for yourself?
- Don't be influenced by negativity.
- Constantly seek advice from people who have more experience, knowledge and success

than you. It will speed up your journey tremendously.

- Don't focus on the past. It does not determine your future.
- Always keep your word.
- Choose to believe that you have the power to create and change anything you really do.
- Complain less and take more action.
- Don't accept mediocrity; choose excellence. Nobody is born mediocre, it's a choice.
- Forgive and let go. It will liberate enormous amount of energy and creativity in you.

"If you find someone who makes you smile, who checks up on you often to see if you are fine, who watches out for you and wants the very best in you, don't let them go. Keep them close and don't take them for granted. Those people are hard to find."

God and Prayer

We must be careful about how we pray and what we request from God because He will provide.

One day a young man went to church to pray. He said: "God, help me. I want to drive a big car with plenty of girls in it, Amen."

God responded. This young man is currently driving a school bus at Joppie Girls Only High School. Next time he prays, he will be more specific.

"It is not the answer that enlightens, but the question." Eugene Ionesco.

Help Others

Never get tired of doing little things for others. Sometimes those little things occupy the biggest part of their heart.

Don't ever try to break someone's heart. Each of us has only one heart, so don't break it.

Stop looking for love where you have lost it.

If you're willing to see positive change in your life, you must be willing to be that change itself.

Unlike in the examination, life has no scope. Life is like a journey on a train with its stations, its changes of routes and its accidents!

At birth, we boarded the train and met our parents, and we believed that they would always travel on our side. However, at some station our parents step down from the train, leaving us on this journey alone. As time goes by, other people board the train. They will be significant, our siblings, friends, children, and even the love of our life.

Many will step down and leave a permanent vacuum. Others will go so unnoticed that we don't realize when they vacated their seats. This train ride will be full of joy, sorrows, fantasy, expectations, hellos, goodbyes and farewells.

The mystery to overcome is: We do not know at which station we, ourselves will step down. So, we must live in the best way - love, forgive and offer the best of who we are.

It is important to do this, because when the time comes for us to step down and leave our seat empty, we should leave behind beautiful memories for those who will continue to travel on the train of life without us. Let's reap success, give lots of love and be happy. More importantly, be thankful for the journey! Try to say thank you to all the passengers on your train.

"Success consists of having a good relationship with all the passengers. That requires that we give the best of ourselves."

Successful people don't reach their destinations and goals alone. In this journey of life, we pass pleasures in pain. There will be sunshine and rain. There will be loss and gain, but we learn to smile again and again.

Always be a reflection of what you'd like to receive. If you want love, give love. If you want the truth, be truthful. If you want respect, give respect. What you give will return to you.

Remember this

The following things should be remembered and be taken care of in life:

- The past cannot be changed, so move on.
- Opinions don't define your reality, so don't be scared.
- Everyone's journey is different, pursue yours.
- Things get better with time, so give them time.
- Positive time creates positive things; change your attitude.
- You fail only if you quit. Don't quit.
- Over thinking will lead only to sadness; answers will come when you least expect them.
- Kindness is free and it is not stupidity. Be kind.
- A smile is contagious, so be contagious.
- What goes around comes around, so help others so that they can help you.
- Judgement is a confession of character. Stop judging people.
- Happiness is found within. Be happy with the little you have.

Delayed Gratification

One day a young lady sat in a bus. At the next stop a loud and grumpy old woman came and sat by her. She squeezed into the seat and bumped her with numerous bags.

A person sitting on the other side of this young lady got upset, asked why she did not speak up and say something. The young lady responded with a smile: "It is not necessary to be rude or argue over something so insignificant. The journey together is so short. I get off at the next bus stop." This response deserves to be written in golden letters.

If we realized that our time here on earth is really that short, then to darken it with quarrels, futile arguments, not giving to others, discontentment and a fault-finding attitude would be a waste of time and energy.

Did someone break your heart? Be calm, the journey is too short. Did someone betray, bully, cheat or humiliate you? Be calm, forgive, the journey is so short. Whatever troubles anyone brings to you, just remember that our journey together is so short.

"Smiling doesn't always mean that you're happy. It simply means that you are a strong person." Anonymous.

Delayed Gratification

No one knows the duration of this journey. No one knows when their stop will come. Our journey together is so short. Let us cherish friends and family. Let us be respectful, kind and forgiving to each other. Let us be filled with gratitude and gladness. If you have ever hurt someone ask for forgiveness. If you have ever hurt me, you already have my forgiveness.

No matter how good or bad your life is, wake up each morning and be thankful that you still have one day, today, this day!

One day I was inspired and motivated by a message which was written on a balloon which was flying high up in the sky in one of the shops in town, during festive season.

The message written reads: “It is not what is outside, but what is inside that takes you to the top.” This simple message has changed my life forever. Life is too short to hate anyone, so forgive often, love someone, smile often and do everything that makes you happy.

Never break the pot that once gave you water. Never bite the hands that once fed you. Never despise the home that once gave you shelter. Never punch holes in the umbrella that once gave you cover.

Never insult the breasts that once gave you fire. If for now you have outgrown their usefulness, leave them intact and go quietly and honourably. For it may be the time and season of breakthrough for others also. Be careful how you close the door.

Never ever bang the door; you may need to walk through that same door tomorrow.

"The most wasted day in my life is the day in which I have not laughed. In this journey of life, we pass pleasures and pains. There will be sunshine and rain. There will be loss and gain, but we must learn to smile again and again." Anonymous.

Don't Take Life Seriously, It's Not Permanent

Nothing is permanent in this world, not even our troubles. Sometimes I enjoy walking in the rain because nobody can see my tears.

If you are beginning to think that what you are doing is very important, you need to take a holiday.

So, taking a holiday does not mean coming to Joppie village for its beauty. No, your holiday can be every day. Take a holiday from your seriousness. Seriousness has come essentially because of your self-importance. You hold yourself as the most important person. Shame on you!

What you must know is that you are like a speck of dust in this existence.

Tomorrow morning if you disappear forever, for sure at Joppie village nobody will miss you. Even six feet down they won't bother much to know you. A handful of people will just remember you from home to cemetery. Isn't it so? Why do you want people to remember you? Because of what?

Everything will happen wonderfully well even if you are not there. Every human being should be aware of this. It does not matter what the whole world says about you. It does not matter how significant is the work you are doing.

You must understand that tomorrow morning the world will be fine without you. The sun will still rise in the east and set in the west. The day will still be 24 hours long.

Just loosen up your life a little bit, laugh a little more. Perhaps the only thing you can do is to cry for your own self, because when you die people, including your next of kin, might not even shed any tears.

Don't be too serious about life. Life is just a game.

One fact of life is that you should stop wasting your time on people who don't deserve your attention. Time spent with people who care about you is time well spent. Don't waste valuable time and energy on things that don't matter; obstacles, challenges and tough times are all part of the deal. So, deal with it and keep moving.

In life, sometimes you outgrow people, particularly your friends. Don't try to bow down to their level. You have just left them in that level. They don't hate you. They just respect you because it is not easy for them to reach your level of thinking.

The tree does not bother about flowers that fall. It is always busy making new flowers blossom. Life is not about what we have lost so far, it's about how we can still grow.

"When someone you love becomes a memory, the memory becomes a treasure." Anonymous.

We suffer more in imagination than in reality. My life has been full of terrible misfortunes, most of which never happened. Everything that irritates you make you understand and know you better. In reality, there nothing such as time, because when you were born, everything was just natural as it is today.

Nothing in life is to be feared. It is only to be understood. People who are afraid of dying are not living. In essence, they are dead alive. If you know where you are going, there is no fear of death.

The most important thing is to be whatever you are without shame or regret. Anyone can look strange to another, but behind all that strangeness there is still a human being.

The longest period between life and death is death. The period which you will stay in your grave is longer than the number of years that you will live. The first hell and heaven are here on earth.

When you are in pain, you are in hell, and when you are at ease with your life, you are in heaven. The second hell and heaven are as promised.

There is a saying that says: The measure of a man is not, “how did he die?” but “how did he live?” not “what did he gain?” but “what did he give?” I personally subscribe to this saying.

Let us learn to count our lives by smiles not tears, to count our age by adding positive values to the lives of others, not years. Do not be sad by people, they will all die. Death is the final proof that everyone is expendable. Always take care of your body, it’s the only place you have to live now.

Life is not measured by the number of breaths we take. Life is measured by the moments that take our breaths away.

Sometimes you have to give up on people. Everyone in your life is meant to be there. But it doesn't mean they're meant to stay.

"Man sacrifices his health to make money, then he sacrifices his money to recuperate his health. He is so anxious about the future, that he doesn't enjoy the present. And he lives as if he's never going to die, and then dies having never really lived." 14th Dalai Lama.

Chapter 4 Stress Management

Nobody was Born Stronger.

In 1992, a young man was favoured to win the 400-meters race in the Barcelona Summer Olympics. However, disappointment came about 250-meters from the finish line. His hamstring tore, he hobbled into a halt, and then fell to the ground in pain.

Stretcher bearers made their way over to him. He knew he had to decide whether to continue or to stop. So, despite the pain, he stood up began to hobble along the track.

Suddenly, a large man pushed through the crowds, fighting back security. The man was his father. "You don't have to do this," he told his weeping son. "Yes, I do!" his son declared. "Well then," replied his dad, "We're going to finish this race together."

The father wrapped his arms around his son and helped him hobble around the track. Shortly before the finish line, the father let go of his son and the son completed the race with a standing ovation from the crowd of over 65,000, all in tears.

Derek Redmond may not have finished first place, but he managed to finish his race!

Despite the pain, despite the tears, he determined to give his all. Motivated by the love so strong of his father who picks him up when he falls. What made his father do that? to leave the stands and meet his son on the tracks? It was the pain on his son's face. His son was hurt, but wanted to finish the race. So, the father came to help him finish the race.

Nobody was born stronger. You only become stronger when you're on the shoulders of another person. You only become stronger when you are surrounded by the people who care about you and love you unconditionally.

God Helps us

God is like that. When we are hurt, and fighting to finish, He comes and helps us. How about you? How is your race? Are you in pain? Are you on the verge of quitting? God wants you to finish strong because He loves you. Will you open your heart to him?

Some of your friends will not want you to go on being successful. They will want you to stay where they are. Friends who don't help you climb will want to see you crawling.

"The less you associate with bad people, the more your life will improve. Any time you tolerate mediocrity in others, it increases your mediocrity. The most

important attribute in successful people is their impatience with negative thinking and negative acting people. As you grow, your associates will change."

Your friends will stretch your vision or choke your dreams. Those that don't increase you will eventually decrease you.

Be Mentally Strong

People who are mentally strong do some of the following things:

- They move on with life. They don't waste time feeling sorry for themselves and what has happened yesterday.
- They embrace change and welcome challenges.
- They stay happy. They don't waste energy on things they that they cannot change or control.
- They are kind, generous, fair and unafraid to speak up.
- They celebrate another people's success as if it's theirs.

Consider this: Never accept counsel from unproductive people. Never discuss your problems with someone incapable of contributing to the solution, because those who never succeeded are always first to tell you that it is impossible. They will teach you how to fail, not how to succeed. Not everyone has a right to comment on your life.

You're certain to get the worst of the bargain when you exchange ideas with the wrong people. Don't follow anyone who's not going anywhere.

With some people, even if you can spend the whole day with them, you'll realise that it was a day well wasted. When you spend time with good people you learn and grow. That's an investment. Be careful where you stop and ask for directions along the road of life. Wise is the person who fortifies his life with the right friendships.

"A mirror reflects a man's face, but what he is really like is shown by the kind of friends he chooses!" my mother once advised me.

Choose Your Associates

The simple but true fact of life is that you become like those with whom you closely associate, for good and for bad.

Note: Do not be mistaken. This applies to the family as well as friends. Yes, do love, appreciate and be thankful for your family, for they will always be your family, no matter what. Just know that they are human first and though they are family to you, they may be a friend to someone else and will fit somewhere in the criteria above.

“In prosperity, our friends know us. In adversity, we know our friends. Never make someone a priority when you are only an option for them.

“If you run with wolves, you will learn to howl. But, if you associate with eagles, you will learn how to soar to great heights.”

If you’re going to achieve excellence in big things, you develop the habit in little matters. Excellence is not an exception, it is a prevailing attitude!” my grandmother once warned me.

Every day is a gift and a new beginning. Whatever glory or pain we had in the past, remember yesterday ended last night.

Accept others for who they are and for the choices they have made even if you have difficulty understanding their beliefs, motives or actions. Try to create a family of friends with whom you can share your hopes, dreams, sorrows and happiness together.

“Whether we die young or old, what matters is the grace to continue to live hereafter!” TB Joshua, SCOAN

There Is Nothing New.

Nothing in life is worth fighting for. Your best clothes are someone's rag, your account balance is someone's donation at a function. Your partner was someone's partner. Every single prostitute you see in a hotel or on the street at night was at some point in time a virgin. So, what is the squabble all about?

Life is too short and small to feel bigger or better than anybody. Steve Jobs once advised. "We are all naked to death. Nothing can save us from it."

I hate to see people who brag about wealth, beauty, intelligence, level of education, fame, material possessions. There's nothing in life that you've achieved that is new to humanity.

The office you occupy today was occupied by someone yesterday and will be occupied by another person tomorrow.

You don't know who that person might be. One of your colleagues, who is now occupying a low position can be your employer tomorrow. Respect them.

Always remember that the people you're likely to pass on your way up a ladder will be the same set of people you're likely to pass on your way down.

Delayed Gratification

When things are fine, some people tend to forget where they come from.

The same people who elected you to office might be the same people who can vote you out one day.

If one day you feel like crying, call me. I don't promise to make you laugh, but I promise you that I can cry with you. If one day you want to run away, don't be afraid to call me. I promise to be there running beside you. If one day you call me and there is no answer, come to me. Perhaps I need you or I'm gone!

Always wear a smile on your face, not because everything is well, but because your smile could be a reason for others to smile.

When people bring your past experiences to others, don't worry. They are intimidated by your progress.

Don't regret your past, just regret the time you've wasted with the wrong people. Pain is inevitable, suffering is optional. Your life is a book, make it the best seller! Damaged people are dangerous because they know that they can survive, with or without you. Life is just an art of drawing without an eraser.

One day we will get separated from each other. We will miss our conversations and everything that we have done together. We will also think of our common goals in life. Days will pass by, months, years, until this contact becomes rare.

"Life is a story that unfolds between a beginning we can no longer remember and an end we know nothing about." Anonymous.

One day our children will see our pictures and ask: "Who are these people?" And we will smile with invisible tears in our eyes, because a heart is touched with strong words and we will say: "It was then that I had the best days of my life with them."

Please note: Just because you are breathing doesn't mean you're alive.

"As you grow older you, you come to realise that life is a series of beginnings and endings. I really believe that much of it is to prepare us for the life's greatest challenges." Zeca Marques, Moroka Swallows FC coach, Sowetan 22nd Oct 2014.

Understanding Depression

What is depression?

Depression is a severely disabling condition that has a profound effect on all aspects of a sufferer's life.

Depression is one of the most common of all psychiatric disorders. It is estimated that 5-10% of the population at any given time is suffering from identifiable depression.

Depression is viewed as an illness that is caused by changes in neurotransmitters in centres of the brain regulating emotion. Depression has a serious impact on family life and productivity in the workplace, increasing sick leave and early retirement. Depression may, at times, be masked behind an alcohol or drug problem.

Depression is an illness that can seriously impair all aspects of person's life, including personal relationships, performance at work and enjoyment of leisure activities.

Cognitive dysfunction (impaired concentration, memory, decision making) is a common feature of depression that can be easily identified in patients with depression but may be overlooked and may persist once other symptoms have resolved.

Symptoms of cognitive dysfunction are predictive of a poor outcome if they are not fully treated and are associated with marked effects on the patients work performance.

One of the features of depression which can make it difficult to diagnose, is that no two people will have exactly the same symptoms associated with the illness. A number of symptoms are, however, commonly seen:

Symptoms

- Depressed mood
- Loss of interest and enjoyment in activities
- Reduced energy, withdrawal, marked tiredness on slight effort
- Poor concentration and attention on task, impaired memory
- Reduced confidence and self-esteem
- Feeling of guilt and unworthiness
- Bleak and pessimistic views of the future
- Ideas or acts of self-destruction or suicide
- Disturbed sleep
- Diminished appetite and weight loss
- Unexplained physical symptoms
- Low libido

Diagnosis

There are a number of different symptoms of depression and these may vary from patient to patient. These symptoms represent a change from the patient's "normal" mood and should have been present most of the time for a period of at least two weeks.

They may develop over a period of weeks or months. The diagnosis of depression is made when the patient has a low mood or a loss of enjoyment and interest in activities coupled with several of the symptoms listed above.

There are no specific blood tests or other investigations that can be used to diagnose depression.

Chapter 5 Marriage

Mother's Message to her Son before Wedding

My son, marriage is for men and not for boys; it is for women, and not for girls. Tomorrow you will have a new mother, a new cook and a new person to share all your secrets with. It will no longer be me, but her.

Love your new mum even more than you love me. Before you walk into her arms forever, let me give you some words to guide you, because I love you.

One day I was arguing with your father. We were screaming; tempers were high. I was angry and he was also angry with me. Then I called him an idiot, fool, stupid, crazy, I called him all sorts of names! He was shocked. He looked at me asking how dare I call him names.

Guess what he did? He didn't raise any of his hands to hit me. He just walked away, banging the door as he went out. My son, if your father had hit me and destroyed my eyes, how will you feel sitting here with me today? How will you regard him as your father? Would you be proud of him or would you be blaming me for calling him names?

Never hit your wife! No matter the provocation. Just walk away and things will be normal. Whenever she offends you, think of this story I just told you now, it could have been your mother. After he left, I was filled with guilt. We slept in the same bed that night and we never spoke to each other. The next day I went to him and pleaded guilty and I did all I could to show him that I was sorry. He finally forgave me. That day I cooked his favourite food, yes, you know he loves vegetables, salads, ox tail and porridge.

After that day, I didn't call him names; my respect for him was ten times stronger.

There is something very important you must always do. My son, listen very carefully, defend your wife. When she is under pressure, stand by her. If your relatives, including myself and your father hate her, it is your duty to make us see her as a Queen. Your uncle never liked me, but your father was always supportive until the perception of your uncle changed.

"My son, cheating on your wife is not good, but at the same time it doesn't mean that you don't love her. It's like hiring a taxi, when you have your own car at home. It saves tyres, ensures long lasting beauty and it also reduces mileage."

There was a day your father was going to host the owner of his company and friends. They were just for them. As was busy cooking, your father went out to buy drinks for them.

I was also curiously listening to what they were saying. One of them said that her girlfriend asked him a difficult question the previous day.

He said his girlfriend asked: "Honey, why is that when a girl had sex with numerous men people hate her and call her names, but when the man does the same, he is a legend?" The man responded: "If a door is opened with more than one key, it becomes a useless door.

No one will want to keep anything important in a room with such door, but if the key opens more than one door, then it's a master key." My son, life is like that.

Your father came back with drinks and other small items.

When the table was set and the food was served, everyone started eating. I remembered that I did not add salt in the food. I was embarrassed.

Your father tasted the food and looked at me. He immediately stood up and turned to our guests. He told them that he instructed his wife last month, not to add salt whenever she is cooking for either visitors or for himself because of health reasons.

He said it in a funny way and everyone laughed, including me. He defended me. The guests understood and he asked me to bring salt and everyone added according to their taste. He managed to eat the food without salt, because of my ignorance.

Now, let me talk to you about love making. I know that in our culture it's a taboo for a mother to talk about sex with her son. You see, sex is a wonderful thing. Do not be surprised if your wife enjoys and needs sex more than you do. That's normal, because of the various aspects that affected you that day. Age is also a factor. There are many factors.

There were days I needed sex more than your father and there were days he needed it more than I. The most important thing is to always try to satisfy the other person, even if you don't feel like it. Don't think of yourself; think of the next person, your wife.

One day your father wanted sex and my body was tired because of the hard manual labour that day. When I got to the bed, he was in the mood. We eventually made love, just to satisfy him not me. During the lovemaking process, I fell asleep. What an embarrassment!

"Your wife is like a baby, sometimes she doesn't know what to say or what to do. Stand up and speak for her. "

My son, sex is best enjoyed when the two parties are physically and mentally ready for it. Sometimes read the mood of your wife, and understand it.

Make it a habit to go everywhere with your wife. Beside your job, move around with her, and introduce her to your relatives.

If someone invites you to his house and told you not to come with your wife, then use your discretion and wisdom. I know that you love mummy, I know you will tell me all your problems and your joys, but now things should be different. Let your wife be the first to know before me. Let her the first to see before me.

When you have problems with her, don't run to me immediately. Wait for a day to pass and then talk to her about it. Report her to nobody, but talk issues out between yourselves.

My son, there was a day when I fainted. One day your father and I visited a farm and we saw a bull having sex with a cow. I asked the farm manager many questions. I said as follows:

Wife: How many times does a bull have sex per day?

Manager: Six times a day.

Wife (I Looked at my husband): You see, that's how it is supposed to be!

Husband: You mean six times a day with the same cow?

Manager: No! It is with different cows every day.

My son, your father looked at me with wide opened eyes, full of laughter. That is the day I collapsed and fainted for a while.

Finally, don't forget to come and visit us every month! I know that you have a happy family. Don't forget to pray every day. My son, mark my words.

Remember, you can't give away your riches if you keep thinking about the hard time you underwent acquiring it.

As a young lady, one day your father made me to laugh my lungs out. It was before we got married. We were just dating each other. We went to a hotel, just for one night. In the morning before we checked out I demanded something to him and I said: "Darling, now that you've managed to get what you wanted from me, you no longer tell me that you love me?" Guess what he has said! He starred at me for a short while and he said: "Have you ever heard or seen a presidential candidate campaigning after winning the elections?"

"Marriage is for men and not for boys, it is for women and not for girls." Anonymous.

My Wife Saved Me.

When I got home that night as my wife served dinner, I held her hand and said to her: "I have something to tell you." She sat down and ate quietly. Immediately I observed the hurt in her eyes.

Suddenly I didn't know how to open my mouth. But I had to let her know what I was thinking. "I want a divorce." I raised the topic calmly.

She didn't seem to be annoyed by my words, instead she asked me softly and said: "Why?"

I avoided her question. This made her angry. She threw away the chopsticks and shouted at me: "You're not a man!"

That night, we didn't talk to each other. She was crying hysterically knew she wanted to find out what might have happened to our marriage, but I could not give her a satisfactory response.

I didn't love her anymore, I just pitied her. She had lost my heart to Jane. With a deep sense of guilt, I drafted a divorce agreement which stated that she should own our beautiful house, our cars and 30% stake of my company. She glanced at it and tore it apart, into very small pieces.

The woman who had spent ten years of her life with me had become a stranger. I felt sorry for wasted time, resources and energy and I could not take back what I had said for I loved Jane so dearly. Finally, she cried loudly in front of me, which was what I had expected to see. To me her cry was actually a kind of relief.

The idea of divorce which had obsessed me for several weeks seemed to be firmer and clearer now.

The next day I came home very late and found her writing something at the table. I didn't have supper but went straight to sleep and fell asleep very fast because I was tired after an eventful day with Jane.

When I woke up, she was still there at the table busy writing something. I just did not care so I turned over and was asleep again.

"Don't break a bird's wing and then tell it to fly. Don't break a heart and tell it to love. Don't break a soul and tell it to be happy. Don't see the worst in a person and expect them to see the best in you. Don't judge a person and expect them to stand by your side. Don't play with fire and expect to stay perfectly safe. Life is about giving

and taking. You cannot expect to give bad and receive good. You cannot expect to give good and receive bad." Najwa Zebian.

In the morning, she presented her divorce conditions as follows:

- She didn't want anything from me, but wanted a month's notice before the divorce.
- She requested that in that one month, we both struggle to live both as normal a life as possible.
- Her reasons were very simple: Our son had his final year examinations in a month's time and she didn't want to disrupt him with our broken marriage. Our son was in Grade 12.

This was agreeable to me. But she had something more, she asked me to recall how I had carried her into out bridal room on our wedding day.

She requested that every day for the month's duration I carry her out of our bedroom to the front door every morning. I thought she was going mad. Just to make our last days together bearable, I accepted her odd request.

One day she said: "My handsome husband, I am not jealous about your relationship with your new wife, Jane. I'm territorial. Jealousy is when you want something that's not yours. Territorial is protecting what's already yours."

I told my new wife, Jane, about my wife's divorce conditions. She laughed loudly and thought it was absurd. "No matter what tricks she applies, she has to face the divorce," she said scornfully.

My wife and I hadn't had any bodily contact since my divorce intention was explicitly expressed. So, when I carried her out on the first day, we both appeared clumsy. Our son clapped behind us.

Our son said: "Daddy is holding Mummy in his arms. And this is a sign of love."

His words brought me a sense of pain. From the bedroom to the sitting room, then to the door, I walked over ten meters with her in my arms. She closed her eyes and said, softly: "Please, don't tell our son about the divorce."

I nodded, feeling somewhat upset. I put her down outside the door. She went to wait for the bus to work. I drove alone to the office.

On the second day, both of us acted much more easily. She leaned on my chest. I could smell the fragrance of her blouse. I realized that I hadn't looked at this woman carefully for a long time. I realized she was not young anymore. There were fine wrinkles on her face, her hair was greying, marriage had taken its toll on her. For a minute, I wondered what I had done to her.

On the fourth day, when I lifted her up, I felt her up. I felt a sense of intimacy returning. This was the woman who had given ten years of her life to me. On the fifth and sixth days, I realized that our sense of intimacy was growing again. I didn't tell Jane about this. It became easier to carry her as the month slipped by.

Perhaps the everyday workout made me stronger. She was choosing what to wear one morning. She tried on quite a few dresses but she could not find the suitable one.

Then she sighed: "All my dresses have grown bigger." I suddenly realized that is the reason why I could carry her more easily.

Suddenly, it hit me. She had buried so much pain and bitterness in her heart. Subconsciously I reached out and touched her head.

Our son came in at the moment and said: "Daddy, it's time to carry mum out." To him, seeing his father carrying his mother out had become an essential part of his life. My wife gestured to our son to come closer and hugged him tightly. I turned my face away because I was afraid I might change my mind at this last minute. I then held her in my arms, walking from the bedroom, through the sitting room, to the hallway.

Her hand surrounded my neck softly and naturally. I held her body tightly; it was just like our wedding day, but her much lighter weight made me sad.

On the last day, when I held her in my arms, I could hardly move a step. Our son had gone to school.

I held tightly and said to her: "I hadn't realized that our life lacked intimacy."

I finally drove to my office. I jumped out swiftly, without locking the door. I was afraid that any delay would make me change my mind.

I walked upstairs. Jane opened the door, and I said to her: "Sorry Jane, I do not want the divorce anymore!" She looked at me, astonished, and then touched my forehead.

"Do you have a fever?" Jane asked. I moved her hand off my head, and I said: "Sorry, Jane, I said I won't divorce.

My marriage life was boring probably because she and I didn't value the details of our lives, not because we didn't love each other anymore. Now I realized that since I carried her into our home on our wedding day, I am supposed to hold her until death do us apart."

She gave me a loud slap and she slammed the door and burst into tears. I walked downstairs and drove away.

At the floral shop on the way, I ordered a bouquet of flowers for my wife. The salesgirl asked me what to write on the card. I smiled and wrote: "I'll carry you out every morning until death do us part."

That evening I arrived home, with flowers in my hands, a smile on my face. I run upstairs, only to find my wife in bed. She was dead.

My wife had been fighting cancer for months and I was too busy with Jane to even notice that.

She knew that she would die soon and she wanted to save me from our son, in case we push through with the divorce. At least, in my eyes of our son, I'm a caring and loving father and husband.

So, find time to be your spouse's best friend and do those little things for each other that build intimacy. Intimacy is the real marriage. Many of life's failures are caused by people who did not realize how close they were to success when they gave up.

Remember, love is the richest of all treasures. Without it, there is nothing; and with it there is everything.

Love never perishes, even if the bones of a lover are ground fine like powder. Just as the perfume of sandalwood does not leave it, even if it is completely ground up. Similarly, the basis of love is the soul, and it is indestructible and therefore eternal.

Beauty can be destroyed, not love.

Some of the things people should know about love are as follows:

- There is nothing much more beautiful in this world than a person who cares.
- All the words ever spoken of love are but drops in the ocean of its feelings.
- I don't care how hard is to be together. Nothing is worse than being apart.
- Love is a choice that you make from moment to moment.
- Respect is as important as love in a relationship.
- When the words disappear, love is all we can hear. When the moments fade, memories are what we hold dear.
- Sometimes the best thing you can do for people you love is to respect their important decisions in life.
- Faith and love are strange, but powerful things; they can work wonders.

- Don't fight what you love; you'll only end up practicing it somewhere else.

"Never cut a tree down in the winter time. Never make a negative decision in the low time. Never make your most important decisions when you are in your worst moods. Wait. Be patient. The storm will pass. Spring will come." Robert H. Schuller.

Rules for a Happy Marriage

Marriage is the only institution where you get the certificate before you can even start writing the examination. All the questions in the examination are compulsory, but marriage alone is optional. It is also an institution where you will never graduate. It is an institution without breaks, free periods, no sick leave and no one is allowed to drop out.

There is no formal education for marriage, and that is the reason why even the illiterates get married. Animals too, get married. Love your spouse more than you love your career, hobbies and money. That other stuff can't love you back.

Raise your words, and not your voice

Your words are more important than your voice. You will damage your throat by screaming. Learn to know each other. Your spouse should know you what you like and what you don't. Be principled. It is the rain that waters flowers and not thunder.

Avoid secretive relationship

If you don't want people to know it, don't do it. You always get angry when people know that you have an extramarital affair. Stop it.

Don't be too secretive, but don't tell him/her everything

Never keep secrets from each other. Secrecy is the enemy of intimacy. Never lie to each other. Lies break trust and trust is the foundation of a strong marriage.

What do you want your husband to do when you keep on telling him that there are men are always proposing love to you?

Remember, it is always cheap commodities that attract more customers. If you have any child outside your marriage wedlock, do not keep it as a secret to your spouse, but at the same time be careful how you tell your spouse.

If you love him/her, set him/her free

The one who loves you will never leave you, because even if there are 1000 reasons to give up, he or she will always find just one reason to hold on.

Why do you marry?

Love is a commitment, not a feeling. Choose to love each other even in those moments when you are struggling to like each other. Always answer the phone when your spouse is calling and when possible, try to put your phones away from yourselves when you are together.

Real love is not based on romance, candlelight dinners and walks along the beach. It is based on respect, compromise, care and trust.

When someone gives you a trust, they are sending a message that says: “Darling, I’m safe when I am with you, no matter what!” Don’t break it. Appreciate it.

Neither both of you be angry at the same time

Be calm when your partner is angry. Don’t invite a third person in your relationship unnecessarily. True love doesn’t happen by accident. It’s deliberate, intentional, purposeful. In the end, it’s real.

Remember that a strong marriage rarely has two strong people at the same time. It’s usually a husband and a wife taking turns, being strong for each other in the moments when the other feels weak. If one of you cries, the other one should comfort him/her. If your spouse is angry with you, just relax.

If you forget that you're a Jew, the Gentiles will remind you

Prioritize what happens in the bedroom. It takes more than sex to build a strong marriage, but it's nearly impossible to build a strong marriage without it.

Try to have sexual intercourse as often as possible, sometimes just for fun. If you forget that you are a man, other men will remind you and if you forget that you're a woman, other women will remind you.

They will use a harsh language. Be warned. Give your best to each other, not your leftovers after you've given your best to everyone else.

Make laughter your soundtrack of your marriage. Share moments of joy, and even in the hard times, find reasons to laugh.

Don't put your marriage on hold while you're raising your kids, or else you will end up with an empty nest and an empty marriage.

Never yell at each other

You can only shout at each only when your house is on fire. There is a lot of difference between human beings and being human. Few understand it. You were loved when you were born. You will also be loved when you die, and in between, you have to manage.

Lose an argument and win a relationship

In every argument, remember that there won't be a "winner" and a "loser." You are partners in everything, so you'll either "win" together or "lose" together.

Work together to find a solution

Arguments are useless and baseless. The relationship is more important than argument. If one of you has to lose an argument, let it be yourself. Laugh as much as possible.

Criticize lovingly and don't bad mouth your spouse in public

Never talk badly about your spouse to other people or vent about them online. Protect your spouse at all times and in all places. When you criticize, do it lovingly and always start with the good things, and then finish with your criticism, lovingly.

Never bring the mistakes of the past

Nobody is perfect. Don't remind each other of your previous mistakes. Look forward, don't look backwards.

Never go to sleep with unsettled argument

If there is an issue which needs to be discussed, let it be done before you go to sleep. If you allow it to pass to the next day, you will not have a peaceful sleep.

Apologise for your mistakes and don't break your spouse's trust on you

When you've made a mistake, admit it and humbly seek for forgiveness. You should be quick to say: "I (was) am wrong. I'm sorry. Please, forgive me, darling!"

When your spouse breaks your trust, give him/her your forgiveness instantly which will promote healing and create an opportunity for trust to be rebuilt.

You should be quick to say: "I love you. I forgive you. Let's move forward with life." At the same time, you should always remember that trust is like an eraser, the more you use it, the smaller it becomes.

You should also connect yourself with friends who will strengthen your marriage. Remove yourself from people who may tempt you to compromise your character.

Don't threaten your spouse with a divorce

In times of disputes, never ever threaten your spouse with divorce. Resolve your differences peacefully, without mentioning divorce. Remember this: A "perfect marriage" is just two imperfect people who are always struggling with their imperfections.

When you have to choose between saying nothing or saying anything, just choose to say nothing every time.

Always wear your wedding ring. It will remind you that you're always connected to your spouse. It will also remind the rest of the world that you're off limits. Be patient with each other. Your spouse is always more important that your schedules.

Make your time of being together a priority. Allow for a consistent "date night". Time is the "currency of relationships". So, consistently invest time into your marriage.

Remember that marriage isn't 50-50, but divorce is 50-50. Marriage has to be 100-100. It's not splitting everything in half, but both partners giving everything they've got.

Don't compare your marriage

Learn from other married people, but don't feel the need to compare your life or your marriage to anyone else's. God's plan for your life is masterfully yours.

Model the kind of marriage that will make your sons want to grow up to be good husbands and your daughters to grow up to be good wives.

Connect into a community of faith. A good church can make a world of difference in your marriage and family. Pray together. Cry together. Celebrate together. Every marriage is stronger with God in the middle of it.

"If you succeed in cheating someone, don't think that the person is a fool - just realize that the person trusted you much more than you deserved." Anonymous.

Chapter 6 Seeds of Kindness

Sweet words are easy to say. Sweet things are easy to buy, but sweet people are difficult to find. Why? Because kindness makes you the most beautiful person in this world, no matter how you look like. How others perceive you is not important, but how you perceive yourself is very important and means everything.

Cruelty to humanity is a curse and too demonic. It is also generational. People who care about others do not expect any reward. The good that you do to fellow human beings today will be rewarded when you least expect it. It can be through your family members.

Do good for others. It will come back in some unexpected ways, and that is karma. The good things that you do for yourself remain with you, but the good that you do for others is forever.

There is nothing more beautiful than someone who goes out of their way to make life easier for others. Happiness isn't about getting what you want all the time.

It's about loving what you have and being grateful for it. Always use your voice for kindness, your ears for compassion, your hands for charity, your mind for truth and your heart for love.

Kindness is still and will always be the strongest force that ties humanity together on this earth.

The seeds of kindness you plant today will one day bloom in the hearts of all the people whose hearts you have touched. People who are kind are also trustworthy. Kind people are always ready to say sorry for any mistake they may make.

Remember: Sorry works when the mistake is made, but not when the trust is broken. So, in life, make mistakes, but never break the trust. Because forgiving is easy, but forgetting and trusting again is something impossible.

Being kind can make you earn the respect of many people, even far beyond the borders and territory of your home town.

Your good deeds might seem invisible, but they leave a trail that is imprinted on the hearts of others. When someone is nasty or treats you poorly, don't take it personally. It says nothing about you, but a lot about them. Mendy Hale asserted that: "There is nothing more beautiful than someone who goes out their way to make life beautiful for others."

"Your beauty attracts the eye, but your kindness and good personality capture the heart. The best makeup is your smile. Listen

to your heart, because wherever your heart is, that is where you'll find your treasure." Anonymous.

Chapter 7 Failure

Main Causes of Failure

Success is not an accident. It is the result of your behaviour which is a function of your attitude and your attitude is your choice. People might wish you all the best in this world, and the honours rest in you. Some will hate you when you work hard and earn everything that this world possesses.

Success is not sexually transmitted or transferred.

Some people dream of success, others make it happen. Some of the main causes of failure in life are as follows:

- Fear

In the moment you want to pursue your goals and start asking yourself questions such as: “What if I fail?” you allow fear to dominate your dreams. It is better to fail by doing something than to excel in doing nothing.

Those who hate you will broadcast your failures, but whispers your successes.

- Unknown destinations.

Someday, somewhere and unfailingly you’ll find yourself, and that can be the happiest or the bitterest hour of your life. Try to search for that unknown place. That is the source of your success.

If you want to buy your own private jet, don't start by checking who else in your household once owned a one. You are not an extension of anyone.

- Once failed.

Just because you failed once doesn't mean that you are going to fail again in everything. Keep trying, hold on and always believe in yourself, because if you don't, who will? We learn a little from our successes, but a lot from our failures.

- Holding back.

Your inner voice will keep small. Ignore it. It hurts more to hold grudges than to forgive. The anger you hold inside damages you, nobody else. Do not be your own prisoner.

Remember: It is better to cry than to be angry because anger hurts others, while tears flow silently through the soul and cleanse the heart.

There are some people who always appear to be angry and continuously look for conflict. Walk away from them. The battle they are fighting isn't with you, it is with themselves. People rain on your parade only because they're jealous of your sun and tired of their shade. Ignore them and pursue your dreams.

"Holding onto anger is like drinking poison and expecting the other person to die." Buddha.

Overcoming Failure

I've found in life that anything worthwhile requires taking a risk. You will fail at some point in your life. Accept it. Sometimes you will lose great things and opportunities. Accept it. You will also embarrass yourself; there is no doubt about it.

If you don't fail, you're not even trying. People will never remember you for your loss, but they will always remember your home runs. They will not even ask you how many years it took you to obtain your degree or diploma. What they can do is to celebrate with you for your victories and achievements.

To make matters worse, even in an interview for a post, they will never ask you the number of years it took you to obtain your degree, diploma or a certificate.

Every failed experiment is one step closer to success. You've got to take risks. Sometimes it's the best way to figure out where you're going.

To get something you have never had, you have to do something you have never done. Remember, if you do what you always did, you will get what you always got. You have to give it your best shot. Sacrifice something in order to get something.

Never be discouraged. Never hold back. Sometimes it may be frightening, but it will also be rewarding, because the chances you take, the people you meet, the people you love, the faith that you have, that's what's going to define you.

You can always build on failure. You should always see failure as a stepping stone. Close the door on the past, because no matter how often you revisit the past, there is nothing new to see. Look forward. Your future is greater than your past.

Even if you don't forget your mistakes, don't dwell on them and let them define who you are. Be patient, but don't wait. Keep on moving.

Time is precious. Make sure that you spend it with the right people, those who don't belittle your ambitions and dreams, people who uplift you and add value to your life and who celebrate with you and cry with you.

The secret of being happy is accepting where you are in life and making the most out of every day. Success is not always about money, but also about the failure. Learn to eat your food as your medicine; otherwise you will have to eat your medicine as your food. Use your failure as a lesson, otherwise you will have to use your success as a failure.

"You must demand more of yourself because every next level of yourself demands a different version of you. Rising above the pain, the challenges, the adversity - That's what makes you grow." Anonymous.

If you don't fight for what you want, don't cry for what you lose. Keep working, keep striving and never give up. If you fall down seven times, get up eight times.

Without commitment, you'll never start, but more importantly, without consistency, you'll never finish. Ease is a greater threat to progress than hardship, so keep moving, keep growing, keep learning.

Everyone experiences failure and rejection. What you might not know is that even the world's most successful celebrities, businessmen, authors, inventors and athletes were once shown the door. The reason they eventually succeeded is that they did not let failure stop them. They steadfastly pursued their dreams, no matter how embarrassed and insignificant, silly or worthless the world made them feel.

Personally, I repeated my standard ten in nineteen eighty-eight, after obtaining an aggregate symbol which was not a requirement for university entrance in nineteen eighty-seven.

Learn to spread your wings so that you can have an idea how far you can fly. Life is not about finding yourself, but about creating yourself.

Success, according to Dr David Molapo, consists of getting up just one more time than you fall. He went on to say that it is like a postage stamp - its usefulness consists in its ability to stick to one thing until it reaches its destination. Everything that has ever been achieved started as an unseen spark in the creative imagination.

The following are some of the people who failed on their way to success. They bounced back strongly to pursue their dreams, passions, aspirations and visions:

- **Nkamo Mowa:** A 32 year old man who was born and bred in Mashile village in Gamphahlele, outside Lebowakgomo in Limpopo in South Africa. He designed and built his own car which has been on the road for the past two weeks (at the time of writing this book). Mowa, who dropped out of school in Grade 8, said that he started out fixing people's radios and television sets before creating his small vehicle last year (2016). The car has been registered with the car authorities. He has named his car Buraki 2, after his favourite movie, which is called Dragon Wars.

- **Moses Ngobeni:** He was born and bred at Giyani, Limpopo province in South Africa. He has created a two-seater road monster last year (2016). He now aims to start mass production of his vehicles. He has designed a BMW318 engine with 250km/h odometer reading maximum speed. His car has been registered with the National Regulatory for Compulsory Specification (NRCS) and it has been awarded a roadworthy certificate by the traffic department.
- **Nelson Mandela:** He initially failed so miserably at ending apartheid, that he was caught and imprisoned. Most would think that being confined between four walls on an island for more than 25 years would kill his spirit - but no. He went on to become President of South Africa, entering the world's history books as South Africa's first black president, South Africa's first democratically elected president, and Nobel Peace Prize winner. He is currently depicted on South Africa's paper currency and remains a symbol of faith, forgiveness and perseverance.
- **Jackson Risava:** He hails from Nkambako village in Limpopo in South Africa. He has

never been in any school to receive formal education, but he had a fleet of buses, ferrying people all over South Africa and even beyond. He started his business by selling cakes from his home as early as the 1930s. He has also contributed a lot in building some schools around his home village, such as Mahwahwa Secondary School. Some of his buses were burned to ashes by protesters for service delivery, but that did not stop him from continuing to service people. He has since passed on, but one of his sons, Ernest, is still following his father's footprints.

- **Joya Varughese:** She is the founder and owner of an independent school in South Africa, Limpopo Province, in Mopani District. The name of the school is St George College. It was not easy for her when she started this famous College, but now it produces excellent results in all grades. It has produced prominent doctors, lawyers, engineers and other professionals.

"You cannot change your life until you change something you do every day." John C Maxwell.

Everybody Dies but Not Everybody Lives

It is not death most of the people fear. It is getting to the end of life, only to realise that you never truly lived.

Everyone is gifted. Your gift is what you were born with. No one gives you your gift. You cannot get it in a college or university. Every human being was born with a gift and has dominion.

Dominion is about controlling the resources through your gift. Our main problem is that our culture doesn't allow it to manifest.

Our culture makes our career more important than our gift. Your prosperity is not in your job or career, but in your gift. Your job is what they pay you to do, but your gift is your area of influence.

Everyone who discovers their gift dominates. A purposeless life is an early death. It is like committing suicide in instalments.

Our parents told us to go to school, get a job, get married, buy a car and a house, pay your bills then you die. That's your whole life in a simple sentence. Your parents never told you that you possess a gift. They educate you to serve them. Your gift is natural.

The number one goal for you in life is employment, whereas the number one goal for God in life is deployment.

Employment is when somebody uses your gift to benefit them. Deployment is when you use your gift to benefit the whole nation and you prosper.

There was a study done in a hospital on one hundred elderly people facing death close to their last breath. They were asked to reflect about their life's biggest regret. Nearly all of them said they regretted not the things they did, but the things they didn't do, the risks they didn't take, the dreams they didn't pursue.

The questions that one should always ask oneself is: "Why do I exist? What is my purpose here on earth?" What might be your last words, just before you die, in case you had the chance to respond? Maybe you will say: "If only I had...!"

Life is not meant to simply work, wait for a weekend, pay rent and car instalment and you die. Every person on this earth has a gift. Do you know yours? Martin Luther King Jr. didn't have a dream, but the dream had him. People don't choose dreams, but dreams choose them.

"I am not afraid of dying, I am afraid of not living while I am alive." Dr Myles Munroe

The question is: "Do you have the courage to grab the dream that picked you, that grips you, or will you let it get away and slip through?"

One day I have learned something about airplanes. I was talking to a pilot and he told me that many of his passengers think that airplanes are dangerous to fly in, but he said that actually it is a lot more dangerous for a plane to stay on the ground.

He said: "Because on the ground the plane starts to rust much faster than it ever would if it was in the air."

This statement makes a lot of sense because a plane was built to live in the skies. And every person was created to live out the dream they have inside them.

Sometimes the saddest loss is to live the life on the ground without taking off. Most of us are afraid of the thief that comes at night to steal our things.

The biggest thief is in your mind. Struggle and criticism are prerequisites for greatness. This is the law of this universe and nobody escapes it.

Remember, there are two types of pains: The pain on your road to success, and the pain of being haunted with regrets. You will fall many times in life. There is no such a thing as a smooth mountain.

We have been given a gift called life, so don't throw it away. Don't allow your past to define you; instead, you were born anew in each moment. So, own it now. Life has no extra time or overtime.

This universe does not owe you anything. Universe means one song. (uni=one and verse=song.) You have a part to play in this song. You can sing soprano, alto, turner or base. The choice is yours.

Be brave, grab that microphone and play.

"The tragedy of life is not death but what we let die inside of us while we live." Norman Cousins.

Take Risks

Take risks in your life. If you win, you can lead, if you lose, you can guide. People are not always what they say, but what they do. So, judge them not from their words, but from their actions.

When a person hurts you, don't feel badly because he has also hurt himself. You are just a casualty. The Law of Nature says that the tree that bears the sweetest fruits gets maximum number of stones.

Take what you can from your life because when life starts taking from you, it takes even your last breath.

In this world, people will always throw stones on the path of your success. It depends on what you make from them - a wall or a bridge?

Challenges makes life interesting, overcoming them makes life meaningful. There is no joy in victory without running the risk of defeat. A path without obstacles leads nowhere.

"Sometimes we need to be hurt in order to grow, fail in order to know, lose in order to gain. Some lessons are learned best through pain." Anonymous.

Past is a nice place to visit, but certainly not a good place to stay. You cannot have a better tomorrow if you are thinking about yesterday all the time. If what you did yesterday still looks big to you even today, then you haven't done much of anything today.

If you don't build your dreams, someone else will hire you to build theirs. If you don't climb the mountain, you can't view the plain and the valley.

Don't leave it idle - use your brain. You are paid for having a brain; you are rewarded for using it intelligently.

It's not what you don't have that limits you, it's what you have but don't know how to use that limits you.

What you fail to learn might teach you a lesson. The difference between a corrupt person and an honest person is: The corrupt person has a price, while the honest person has a value. Honesty is an expensive gift; don't expect it from cheap people.

"Both tears and sweat are wet and salty, but they render a different result. Tears will get you sympathy, but sweat will get you change or progress." Jesse Jackson.

Chapter 8 Leadership and Management

Leadership and Management Defined

Not all managers are good leaders and not all leaders are good managers. Management is paperwork, while leadership is people work.

"Leadership is the capacity to inspire others through inspiration, guided by passion, which is produced by vision which is a result of purpose." Myles Munroe.

Leadership is a choice you make and not a position you sit. Therefore, leadership cannot be awarded, appointed, bestowed or be given. Anyone can choose to become a leader wherever he is. You can make a difference no matter where you are.

A position doesn't make a leader but a leader does. Leadership is learned daily, not in a day. It is an ongoing process, not a one-time payment or event.

Secure and mature leadership are not threatened by the successful development of those whom they lead. True leaders focus on developing others.

Are leaders born or made? This is the question which many people ask as they address people on leadership.

Leaders admit faults, but never make excuses. Immature leaders lead first, then they listen afterwards, if they listen at all. Experienced leaders listen before they lead.

Don't measure the success of your army with the paces of the fastest soldiers. As a leader, don't try to move fast, such that your followers can't follow.

If you think you are leading, and nobody is following, you're just taking a walk. Leadership involves the whole person, and therefore cannot be relegated to our "professional compartment" of our lives.

True leaders are quick to listen, slow to speak and slow to be angry. (James 1:19 KJV) He does not need others to motivate him, but he motivates himself.

Leadership is therefore intrinsic and not extrinsic. In other words, leadership comes from inside and from outside.

"Leaders are not just born to the role. They are born, then made-and sometimes unmade by their own actions. A leader who is not in tune with the followership will become a leader in limbo." Reuel J Khoza.

Leadership is deployment and not employment

Entertainment and relaxation are not the principal goals of a true leader, because no time is truly his. The success of leadership is measured by the people you "produce", and not the number of the people who follow you.

True leadership measures his success and effectiveness by the diminishing degree of his followers' dependency on him – the less they need him, the more effective he is. We teach our kids how to cook, an even how to read and write. Immediately they know how to cook and how to read and write without our supervision, the happier we become.

If your presence is required for your organisation to function, then your leadership is likely weak. True leader should always possess natural wisdom, which is more important than your academic accomplishment.

You might be having highest academic accomplishments or honour, but still be foolish.

Natural wisdom comes from God. Before you lead, request Him to provide you with wisdom.

Any leadership without the presence of the Father is useless or deemed to fail dismally.

Five negative issues that can trip a leader are as follows:

- Greed.
- Guilt
- Jealousy
- Anger
- Corruption

"Greed is like drinking salty water, the more you drink, the more you want." PLO Lumumba

Management is a position one holds. Management can be relegated to one's academic accomplishments, unlike leadership. You can be become a leader even if you are not educated.

Difference between leaders and managers

Leader	Manager
1.Innovates	1.Imitates
2.Is an original copy	2.Is a photo copy
3.Implements his ideas	3.Always seeks approval
4.No office hours	4.Has office hours
5.does people work	5.does paperwork

"Leadership is not about position but disposition, it is not about manipulation but emancipation, it is not about power but empowerment." Anonymous.

Qualities of a True Leader.

A true leader manages the following:

Time

This is the most critical aspect to be managed. Political leadership can hardly manage time, and this might be the reason why some of our projects fail dismally. I, personally (for more than twenty years as an active party politician) do not remember a single gathering where the so-called leaders arrived in time for their meetings.

If you fail to manage time, time will manage you.

A true leader knows that: "There is a time for everything, and a season for every activity under heaven." Ecclesiastes 3:1 Holy Bible (NIV)

Some leaders want to be in power forever. It is incorrect. Until we can manage time, we can manage nothing else. No matter how many nice words you may use for your late arrival, your audience will be angry with you until you finish addressing them. Late arrival to gatherings is a deadly disease, a curse and is also contagious. Be careful because it is generational. Your corpse will also anger mourners because it will also be delivered late by the undertaker.

"Nobody is busier than another. It's just a matter of priorities and having integrity." Anonymous

Choice of words (Diction)

It is not what you say what matters, but how you say it. Remember: An unguarded word always destroys its speaker. Words hurt more than actions do, they hit you deep in your heart and the pain will never go away. Not even a 'sorry' can heal the hurt caused by words.

Words do not have the power to hurt you, unless the person who said them means a lot you. It does not matter how right or wrong you are, you have no right to offend people by virtue of being either their leader or manager. Respect them.

Be careful with your words, as a human being, because once they are said, they can be only be forgiven, not forgotten.

Sometimes it is very beautiful to stay silent when someone expects you to be enraged. Sometimes you have to be quiet to heard. Good leaders think before they speak, no matter how excited or outraged they might appear. Do not allow people to have more authority over you that their silence leaves you questioning your worth.

Not everything that can be seen or heard is worth commenting. Quiet people have the loudest minds.

"I've learned that people will forget what you said, people will forget what you did, but people will never forget how you made them feel." Maya Angelou.

Energy

Don't waste your energy on something insignificant. Today is today, not tomorrow, but today. Stop wasting your energy about tomorrow. Tomorrow will be a yesterday of the day after tomorrow.

We worry a lot about tomorrow as though it's promised. Who promised you that you will see tomorrow? Anything that consumes you mind controls your life. Don't worry about your future. You can't control it. Focus on the current moment and what you can do now.

Sometimes you have to accept the fact that certain things will never go back to how they use to be. Enjoy life today; yesterday is gone and tomorrow may never come.

True leaders are also aware that some people are just people who enjoy disturbing the smooth running of their organisation. Not everything people do needs your attention.

Relationships

The quality of your happiness lies in your relationship. Ask yourself if what you are doing today is getting you closer to where you want to be tomorrow.

Personally, I want to be your favourite hello and your hardest goodbye. You have to let people go. Not everyone who is in your life is meant to be forever in your journey of life. Not all of them are meant to stay until the end.

Don't blame people for disappointing you, blame yourself for expecting too much from them. In any relationship, a friend who frowns is better than an enemy who smiles.

"The mark of great sportsmen is not how good they are at their best, but how good they are at their worst." Martina Navratilova.

Priorities

Put first things first. Start by doing things which will make you happy. Remember: Never regret things that made you smile. Quitting should be the last option, but when you feel like quitting think about why you started.

"Things which matter most must never be at the mercy of things which matter least." Steven R Covey.

Levels of Leadership

In his *The 5 Levels of Leadership*, John C Maxwell identifies five levels of leadership as follows:

Level 1: Position.

This is the entry level. It is the lowest level of leadership. People follow you because they have to. The only influence a positional leader has is that which comes with the job title.

In order to lead, these leaders rely on instructions and rules. Position level requires no leadership ability, as long as you meet the relevant criteria for the position.

People who make it to level 1 may be bosses, but they are never leaders. They have subordinates, not team members. They rely on rules, regulations, policies, and organization charts to control their people. Their people will only follow them within the stated boundaries of their authority. Position is the only level that does not require ability and effort to achieve. Anyone can be appointed to any position.

Level 2: Permission.

People follow you because they want to. It is based on relationship. People like you, not because of your position. Your good character attracts people. Good relationship is a foundation for good leadership. They sometimes invite you to motivate them. When you like people and treat them like individuals who have value, you begin to develop influence with them. You can like people without leading them, but you cannot lead people well without liking them.

Level 3: Production.

People follow you because of what you have done for the organisation. These leaders are the change agents. They can tackle tough problems and face thorny issues. They produce other leaders. This based on results.

Level 4: People development.

People follow you because of what you have done for them. They empower others and change their lives. These leaders use their position, relationships, and productivity to invest in their followers and develop them until those followers become leaders in their own right. Leaders reproduce themselves.

Level 5: Pinnacle.

People follow you because of who you are and what you represent. Only naturally gifted leaders ever make it to this highest level. These leaders create opportunities that other leaders don't. They create legacy in what they do.

"If you believe that the position makes the leader, you will have a hard time becoming a good leader." John C Maxwell.

Leadership Principles Leaders Can Learn From Lions

What is the first thing that comes to your mind when you see a lion or hear about it? Is it its strength? Is it its fierceness and its boldness? Is it its regal, majestic bearing? Or is it its magnificent appearance?

Whatever it is you know about the lion, you will still have to agree that it is a special animal. In fact, it is so special that it is referred to as the "King of the Jungle" (even though it is mostly found in grassland).

The lion, as an animal is one that every leader and aspiring leader should strive to learn from.

Make yourself be heard

Fact 1: A lion's roar can be heard from five miles away.

Lesson: Make yourself be heard

You may have good intentions in mind, but if you don't say them out, nobody will know how noble they are.

There are plenty of animals that are bigger and stronger and have more stamina than the lion.

There are animals that are faster; there are animals that are even better hunters, but what makes the lion arguably the most fearsome animal to walk the earth is its voice. Its voice is its reputation.

Many of us have not met Nelson Mandela or Oliver Tambo, but we know about them because they had statements to make and they made those statements.

It is important for you to know that the statement you make is not just about what you say. The things you do and your character are part of your reputation.

The lion knows that its roar precedes it everywhere it goes. That is why it is the epitome of boldness.

If you develop your reputation properly, your boldness will increase. Never make the mistake of believing that your friends, or siblings or neighbours or co-workers should be able to read your mind.

There is nothing to be gained from sparing yourself. Try to express yourself. Even if you know that you are not extroverted, you can write. If you know that you have a talent, or gift, use it. Go out and make friends, a recluse is of no use to anyone. .

"Unless the tortoise sticks its head out of its shell it cannot go anywhere." African proverb.

Interact with others

Fact 2: Lions are very social animals, they form groups called Prides with sometimes as many as forty individuals in a Pride.

Lesson: Interact with others so that you can get better and grow.

Your physical growth is automatic, but mental growth is not. Some leaders believe that life is a road that should be travelled alone and that the task of leadership is a burden that cannot be shared, which is not correct.

While these assertions are true to some extent, we all still have to recognize that there is a reason that we have family members, friends, co-workers, bosses, mentors, followers or even employees.

They are not just there because they are our blood, or they have something to gain from us.

They are there to rejoice with us in happy moments, to share sorrows with, to impart knowledge to us and to help us in our highways of life.

One fascinating thing about a Pride of lions is that other females are always ready to help a female to babysit her cubs when she goes hunting.

We should recognise that the reason why the sea is so big is that it has many small rivers, streams, rivulets feeding it.

The leader should recognize himself as a river feeding others and being fed by others in turn. A river which isolates itself, will feeds nothing and it will eventually start to stink or dry up.

The leader should always embrace the popular acronym: TEAM-Together Everyone Achieves More.

There is a saying in Xitsonga language*: "Khongoloti i khongoloti hikokwalaho ka swingwavila swa rona,"* which means a chief cannot be a chief without his subjects or followers.

When you interact with people you learn more and you also grow.

John Donne, a poet, wrote a poem titled: No Man Is an Island. The poem reads:

"No man is an island,

Entire of itself;

Every man is a piece of the continent,

A part of the main.

If a clod be washed away by the sea, Europe is the less

As well as the promontory were..."

Human beings do not thrive when isolated from others.

"Do not build fortresses to protect yourself-isolation is dangerous. " Robert Greene.

Find Time to Relax

Fact 3: A lion can spend up to 20 hours a day sleeping.

Lesson: There is a difference between a leader and a slave.

The temptation to work and work until one collapses from sheer exhaustion has never been greater than it is in our society.

Every day when we wake up, there are always targets to meet, meetings to participate in, dates to keep and objectives to realize. As a result, we are tempted to work and work as slaves.

Delayed Gratification

We give freely to our activities and people around us, yet we fail to realize that we need time for ourselves. We are constantly burnt out and worn out yet we do not see the need to relax.

There is an expression in Xitsonga language which says: *"Ntirho wa hosi wu dlayile xiphukuphuku,"* meaning, do not overwork for sake of pleasing your bosses, because you will get exhausted and die. Get time to relax.

Let us not slave ourselves away like worker bees, and not enjoy the short time we have to live. Learn from the lion who knows that every day it must eat, yet still sleeps for more than half a day. In spite of this perceived irresponsibility, the lion never goes hungry. It starts hunting when it still has enough energy, not when it is extremely hungry. Prepare your meal when you are not excessively hungry.

The irony of work is that it never finishes, the more you work, the more you still have to work. The work you are working now was once worked by others, and they are now gone but the work still needs to be done. Remember: Everything that you do was once done by others. It's not new.

In the insect kingdom, workers are the ones that have nothing else to do but work. One of the marks of the leader is that he does not soil his hands with work meant for his followers.

If you want to have an enjoyable life, learn to not let activity dominate your life. Find time to relax.

Create your own time with your beloved ones for relaxation and fun. Travel to an area with which you are not even familiar. Sometimes a lion can walk for a very long distance in order to search for a Pride with whom it can have time and relax together.

How much sleep does the average adult need? For most adults, seven to eight hours a night appears to be the best amount of sleep.

Sleeping is the best cure for weariness. Relax, don't worry much about your work, because even tomorrow is still another day. Your work will never get finished, but you will.

"Work for a cause, not for applause. Live your life to express not to impress. Don't strive to make your presence noticed, just make your absence felt." Anonymous.

Learn how to share

Fact 4: Lions rarely eat the entire prey, they usually leave leftovers for other animals like hyenas and vultures.

Lesson: The ability to share is the hallmark of a leader.

Every leader has a group of people following him. It is the duty of the leader to ensure that those followers get a fair distribution of every benefit that accrues to the organization.

Being a leader is not just the ability to give orders and commands, or share out work, it is also the ability to motivate.

There is nothing that can motivate like rewards and incentives. A true leader does not hold those things back. Workers should sometimes be given tokens of appreciations of their performances.

If you want to be respected, you must be willing to give freely of yourself to others. It is hard to imagine that the lion, in spite of its voracious appetite and the amount of food needed to satisfy its massive body needs, is still considerate enough to leave leftovers for carrion eaters.

There is no level of need that should prevent you from giving to others. No act of kindness, no matter how small is ever wasted.

What we do for ourselves remains with us, but what we do for others is eternal and lives forever. We make a living by what we get, but we make life by what we give. We rise by lifting others. Only by giving we are able to receive more than we already have, and giving opens the way for receiving.

If you help others to achieve what they want in life, you will also achieve what you want. No one has become poor from giving. The willingness to share does not make one charitable; it makes one free. The heart that gives gathers.

The greatest gift you can give someone is your time, because when you give your time, you are giving a portion of your life that you will never get back.

The lion gives the leftovers to other animals, which do not even belong to its family - the cat family. No leader in history has ever been honoured for what he received. Honour has been the reward for what he gave.

The law of giving is very simple. If you want joy, give joy. If love is what you seek, offer love.

"The old man that eats without consideration for the people around him, will carry his load home by himself." Yoruba proverb.

Learn How to Delegate Responsibility

Fact 5: Male lions defend the Pride's territory while females go to hunt. Despite this the male gets to eat first.

Lesson: Learn how to Delegate Responsibility.

This is the main reason why humans have manpower and not horsepower. There is also a reason why human beings do not have the ability to teleport.

Unless you have the ability to split yourself, you have to accept that you cannot do everything or be everywhere at the same time. Even if you are a "Man of steel," there are not enough hours in the day to do everything that should be done. Therefore, you have to learn to give some tasks to others to do.

Some people are staunch believers in the maxim, "if want anything to be done right, you have to do it yourself." Similarly, the Xitsonga proverb says*:" Mhisi yi pfumarile timhondzo hi ku rhumisa."*

Unfortunately, taking this maxim literally is a sure way to get burnout, high blood pressure and nervous breakdown. One interesting fact is that despite the fact that the female makes the kill she brings it for the male to eat first.

What we can all learn from this is that giving a task to somebody else to do for you doesn't mean that you're giving them room to undermine your authority. It means that you recognize that person's ability and skills and you recognize such a person as useful and important to the organization.

If the project is successful it is still the leader who gets most of the credit, so a true leader should not be paranoid about sharing duties out.

One thing we should take note of is that the lion does not roll over and go to sleep when its mate goes to hunt. It has work that it also does.

Do not give all your work and then laze about all day. That is not delegation of duty. It is laziness and such action leads to lack of respect from your followers. Do not be like the blacksmith who had too many irons in the fire and did not know which one to work on first.

As a leader, learn to delegate authority and not responsibility.

"Surround yourself with the best people you can find, delegate authority and don't interfere as long as the policy you've decided upon is being carried out." Ronald Reagan.

Mate at Home

Fact 6: During mating, the male and female are constantly together, and they usually do not eat, they fast. When the female is finally in the mood, she lies down and the male mounts her. A pair of lions can mate 40 times in a day. During mating, they hide from the Pride.

Just like human beings, lions greet each other every day by rubbing. The rubbing can be quite vigorous and forceful. Males will sometimes knock each other over when they rub. This rubbing serves a purpose.

There are scent glands on the corners of the mouth. Rubbing deposits this scent on the other lion. This scent is kind like a mark of bonding ownership, and the other lion will relish this mark.

Lesson: Regardless of the leader's workload, mating should be the first priority at home. It is also the best stress reliever ever.

There is nothing wrong with making love during the day and openly, but make sure that your kids do not see you.

If you don't laugh during sex at least once, you're having sex with the wrong person. Lions hide from the Pride during this activity. Let us also practice the same. Sex is healthier than physical exercises.

Some leaders do not have a stable relationship with their spouses, primarily because they are always tired. They don't even have time for love making.

"As you grow older you will realise that you have two hands. One for helping yourself, and the other for helping others." Audrey Hepburn.

Leadership Concepts

In order to lead effectively, people have used sayings, slogans, proverbs and their own beliefs. Some of them are as follows:

- Any leadership without the presence of God is useless or doomed to fail dismally.
- The ultimate measure of a man is not where he stands in moments of comfort, but where he stands at times of challenges and controversy. Martin Luther King Jnr.
- The higher the monkey climbs, the more he shows his tail. John Wycliffe
- He who pays the piper calls the tune.
- When money speaks, truth keeps silent. Russian Proverb
- A "No" uttered from the deepest conviction is better than a "Yes" merely uttered to please, or worse, to avoid trouble. Mahatma Gandhi

- If your actions inspire others to dream more, learn more, do more, and become more, you are a leader. John Quincy Adams
- To handle yourself, use your head, to handle others, use your heart. Eleanor Roosevelt
- Never give an order that can't be obeyed. Douglas MacArthur
- Example is not the main thing in influencing others. It is the only thing. Albert Schweiter
- Leaders must be close enough to relate to others, but far enough ahead to motivate them. John C Maxwell
- I am not afraid of an army of lions led by a sheep, I am afraid of an army of sheep led by a lion. Alexander the Great
- Management is doing things right, leadership is doing the right thing. Peter Drucker
- Have faith in humanity. Humanity is like an ocean; if a few drops of the ocean are dirty, the whole ocean doesn't become dirty. Mahatma Gandhi
- One man with courage is a majority.
- Take care of your character and your reputation will take care of itself.
- What people don't understand they call names, and what they understand they destroy. TB Joshua
- History will absolve me. Fidel Castro

Delayed Gratification

- Even if you are a minority of one, the truth is the truth. Mahatma Gandhi
- Leaders inspire, they create opportunities for others and not themselves. They are like fruit trees. Fruit trees bear fruit, but they do not eat their own fruit.
- Let us inspire others before we expire.
- Even if you regard yourself as a dwarf, try to tower above giants.
- We are all like tea bags, you will never know your strength until you are in hot water.
- A joy shared is a joy doubled, but a pain shared is a pain halved. Max Sisulu
- No sun outlasts its sunset, but it will rise again and bring the dawn. Maya Angelou
- In a winter season, a hot day does not make a summer season, it will still be winter.
- A leader is useless when he acts against the promptings of his own conscience. Mahatma Gandhi
- We elect hyenas to take care of the goats, and when the goats disappear we wonder why. PLO Lumumba
- Leadership success is measured by the success of your successor. Myles Munroe
- No matter how overcrowded the sky might be with stars, I may find myself among them if I don't give up in life.

- Love affair with knowledge will never end in a heart break.
- The darkest hour is just before dawn.
- Never fear shadows for they signify that there is a light nearby.
- Fools multiply when wise men are silent.
- Evil men succeed when righteous men do nothing.
- Darkness rules when light is absent.
- Even if you fall on your face, you're still moving forward. Victor Kiam
- Never fight with a pig, you both get dirty and the pig enjoys it.
- We may dodge our responsibility but we may not dodge the consequences of dodging our responsibilities.
- Problems reign when solutions are ignored.
- You can chain me, you can torture me, you can destroy this body, but you will never imprison my mind. Mahatma Gandhi.

"Money is numbers and numbers never end. If it takes money to be happy, your search for happiness will never end." Bob Marley.

Chapter 9 The Basic Johari Window

Two American psychologists, namely Joseph Luft and Harry Ingham devised a model in 1955, while researching group dynamics at the University of California Los Angeles. They named this model Johari Window.

The Johari Window model is a simple and useful tool for illustrating and improving self-awareness, and mutual understanding between individuals within a group, personal development and understanding relationships. They are called **The Basic Johari Window** or **The Four Selves.**

The Public Self/Open persona

The public self is the part of ourselves that we are happy to share with others and discuss openly.

Thus, you and I both see and can talk openly about this 'me' and gain a common view of who I am in this element.

It is about what I and you see in me, for example, my talent or gift of playing football.

The Private Self /Hidden Self/Naïve Persona

There are parts of ourselves that are too private to share with others. We hide these away and refuse to discuss them with other people or even expose them in any way.

Private elements may be too embarrassing or shameful in some way. They may be fearful or seek to avoid being discussed for reasons of vulnerability.

Between the Public and Private selves, there are partly private, partly public aspects of ourselves that we are prepared to share only with the trusted others.

It's about what you do not see in me. I am the only person who sees them, for example, my health.

The Blind Self

They often assume that the public and private selves are all that we are. However, the views that others have of us may be different from those we have of ourselves. For example, a person who considers himself as intelligent may be viewed as an arrogant and socially ignorant by others.

Our Blind Self may remain blind because others will not discuss this part of us for a range of reasons.

Perhaps they realize that we would be unable to accept what they see. Perhaps they have tried to discuss this and we have been so blind that we assume their values are invalid. They may also withhold this information as it gives them power over us.

This self is about what I do not see in me. For example, people know your weaknesses, whereas you don't know them.

The Undiscovered Self/The Secret Persona

Finally, the fourth self is one which neither we nor other people see. This Undiscovered Self may include both good and bad things that may remain forever undiscovered or may include both good and bad things that may one day be discovered, entering the private, blind or maybe even public self.

Nobody knows what tomorrow will bring for us. It is known only by God.

Chapter 10 Why Worry?

When people hurt you over and over again, think of them as sandpaper. They scratch you and hurt you, but later, you will be shining and polished while they end up being useless.

There comes a time where you have to choose between turning the page and closing the book.

It is sometimes sad when people who gave you the best memories become a memory.

The only difference between a bad day and a good day is your attitude. I love people who can make me laugh during the moments when I feel like I can't even smile.

It's not about who is real to your face, but it's about who stays real behind your back. Whoever is trying to bring you down is already below you. Never ever start your day with the broken pieces of yesterday. Try to regard every day as the first day of your life.

I am happy to be me. I am not perfect, but I am honest and always trying to be happy. I will never try to be something I am not, and I am not here on earth to impress anyone else. I am me.

Smiling always increases your face value. Smile even when it hurts. Reasons to cry will always prevail in life.

There is something I don't understand about happiness and sadness. Why can't we laugh at the same joke again, but we cry at the same problem again?

Stop making time for people who don't have time for you. Treat people the way they treat you and stop over-exerting yourself by giving love where it's not returned.

Stop calling people who don't call you, and visiting people who don't even know where you live.

You will make yourself emotional bankrupt if you always think about people who don't think of you. Your existence is nothing to them.

Most importantly, surround yourself with people who don't see you as an option. There is nothing worse than people who treat you as though you are replaceable.

"Mirror is my best friend, because when I cry it never laughs." Charlie Chaplain.

Life is different enough without having to beg people for their love and attention. The least you can do for yourself is to surround yourself with people who genuinely love and care about you.

Surround yourself with people who can laugh with you and not at you, who can also cry with you and not laugh for your downfall.

Delayed Gratification

As soon as the plane lands at the airport, there is another plane taking off from that airport, and others lined up to take off too.

They all leave for different destinations and even back to the airport you departed. This is the way life is. When you think that you have "arrived" you find others are taking off, some from where you are coming from and others to other activities.

There are people crying day and night for lack of children and yet others are crying day and night because of the ill behaviour of their children.

I have met people depressed for not having married. There are people who are sick and tired for being married to a wrong person. Some are without jobs, whereas others are depressed of their jobs.

I have seen parents very worried on how their kids will perform in examinations, while others are worried on how to take who have performed well to tertiary institutions. This is life. We will never have it all and it's like chasing the wind.

Learn to be content in every situation. Enjoy what you have and where you are. Instead of always being in a marathon trying to get it all, it's important to take frequent pauses and reflect.

If your problems can be solved don't worry, even if they cannot be solved, don't worry. If you are right in any situation, then there is no need to get angry. If you are wrong, you don't have any right to get angry.

I have learned that there is no need to tell a person that you love him/her because it shows. Deeds speak. Being kind is more important than being right in life. Your money or your worth will not buy you wisdom. Having a child fall asleep in your arms is one of the most peaceful feelings in the world!

Never think hard about the past, it brings tears, and don't think more about the future, it brings fear. Live this moment with a smile, it brings cheer. Every test in our life makes us better or bitter.

"Never say no, to a gift from a child. I have also learned with sadness that life is like a roll of toilet paper. The closer it gets to the end, the faster it goes." Anonymous.

Chapter 11 Works Consulted

1. Covey, Steven R (2011): The 3rd Alternative. Simon & Schuster Ltd
2. Cousins, Norman (1979): Anatomy of an illness as perceived by the patient. Delacorte Press.
3. De Angelis, Barbara (1991): The Secrets about Men Every Woman Should Know. Random House Publishing Group.
4. Green, Robert (1998): The 48 Laws of Power. Profile Books Ltd, Viking, a Division of Penguin Putnam Inc.
5. Holy Bible (2015): New International Version. Biblica Printers, USA
6. Ionesco, Eugene (1958): The Bald Soprano and other stories. Grove/Atlantic, Incorporated.
7. Khoza, RJ (2011): Attuned Leadership. Penguin Group, publishers.
8. Maskona, Maxwell (2014): Pressing On .PCN Printers cc
9. Mason, John (2016): Fall seven times stand up eight. Christian Art Publishers.
10. Maxwell, John C (2008): The 4 Pillars of Leadership. Thomas Nelson, Inc. (2012): The 15 Invaluable Laws of Growth. Grand Central

Publishing. (2011): The 5 Levels of Leadership. Thomas Nelson, Inc.
11. Monroe, Myles (1991): Understanding Your Potential. Worldwide Distribution. USA.
12. Schuller, Robert H (2000): Turning Hurts into Halos.Indigo Books.
13. Wilde, Oscar (1888): The Happy Prince and other Tales. Penguin Books.
14. Worldscapes (1997): A Collection of Verse Compiled by Robin Malan. Oxford University Press, Southern Africa.
15. Zebian, Najwa (2016): Mind Platter. Amazon

EXTRACTS FROM PRESENTATIONS, PAMPHLETS AND INTERVIEWS

1. Barack Obama: www.google.co.za
2. Bob Marley: www.google.co.za
3. Myles Monroe: www.sabc.co.za 24 May 2012 with Vuyo Mbuli
4. Patrick Loch Otieno Lumumba: Abram Tiro Memorial Lecture, University of Limpopo, Republic South Africa on the 08th September 2017, Tiro Hall.
5. TB Joshua: www.google.co.za/you tube.com
6. Jesse Jackson: www.google.co.za/youtube.com
7. WHO, October (www.who.int/mediacentre/factsheets/fs369/en/index.htm)

About the Editor

Mr. William Jenkins was born in Ottawa, Canada in 1932. He became a computer programmer and worked in that field for 45 years. Subsequently, he sold residential real estate and then wrote and published a few mystery stories for middle-school children.

After finding publishing using Createspace particularly easy, he began publishing books for others as a free service. There is no charge for the publishing and editing service. See his website http://williamjenkins.ca.

He is especially interested in publishing stories and poems from students. A few students from South Africa have submitted their writing.

If you are a teacher or student, submit your writing to williamhenryjenkins@gmail.com by email.

Delayed Gratification

85656121R00113

Made in the USA
Columbia, SC
20 December 2017